HOME POOL

Also by Bruce Ducker

HOME POOL

STORIES OF FLY FISHING AND LESSER PASSIONS

Bruce Ducker
Art by Duke Beardsley

STACKPOLE
BOOKS

Published by
STACKPOLE BOOKS
5067 Ritter Road
Mechanicsburg, PA 17055
www.stackpolebooks.com

Printed in the United States of America

First edition

10 9 8 7 6 5 4 3 2 1

Cover design by Caroline Stover
Cover art by Duke Beardsley

Library of Congress Cataloging-in-Publication Data

Ducker, Bruce.
  Home pool : stories of fly fishing and lesser passions / Bruce Ducker ;
art by Duke Beardsley. — 1st ed.
    p. cm.
  ISBN-13: 978-0-8117-0386-4
  ISBN-10: 0-8117-0386-X
  1. Fishing stories, American. 2. Fly fishing—Fiction. I. Title.
  PS3554.U267H66 2008
  813'.54—dc22
                                    2007046774

To the places I've fished—

the Roaring Fork, Frying Pan, Blue, Crystal, Gunnison,
Big Hole, Big Horn, Snake, Little Wood, Boise, Bow,
Animas, Cache la Poudre; Iceland's Laxa Alvadal, the
Laramie, the headwaters of the Amazon, the Tongue of
Wyoming and the Tongue of the Ocean; the creeks of
Wigwam, Sopris, Bellows, and Silver, and of Armstrong,
Nelson, and Hart; the Blackfoot, Madison, Gallatin,
Yellowstone, Easter Elchies on the Spey; the Battenkill, Belle
Fourche, White, Marvine, Pecos and Piedra; the Coca in the
Andes, the Talbac in Belize, and the Blackwater in County
Cork; the Ruby, Green, Missouri, and the Elk; the tranquil
Yampa and the mighty Huerfano; South Andros, Ascenscion
Bay, Punta Arena, the Little Snake, Henry's Fork, and the
Idaho Snake; the Teton, Uncompahgre, San Miguel,
Colorado, North Platte, Arkansas, Rio Grande; the
Housatanic, Clark's Fork, Beaverhead, the Salmon and the
Selway; Ambergris, Chetumal, Bahia de Drake; the
mysterious Big Lost; uncounted mountain lakes and twice
as many unnamed streams—

and the pals who have fished them with me:
Smitty, Charlie, George, Tim, Fred, Airman John, Sam,
Henry, Peter, Tom, Greg, Dave, Marsh, Foster, Duke, Wes . . .

CONTENTS

ARTWORK

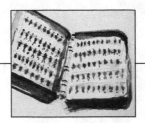

THE SPECTER AT GRIZZLY HACKLE

A lec and Elyse Gardiner were what the older generation called an attractive couple. He was mannerly, bright—if anything, a dot too bright—and capable. He selected his clothes in a style befitting his place: off-the-rack suits from good stores. His elders considered him too young for bespoke tailoring, and they were pleased that he seemed to agree.

And Elyse was every inch his match. Slender, well groomed, witty in a quiet way. She did have her own opinions, and they would slip out in conversation. That is how modern women act. High spirited, one doyenne called her. Elyse wore her black hair to her shoulders, her legs were long as a colt's, and she played a sound game of tennis. Not competitive, simply good, social tennis.

The Gardiners had moved to town ten years ago. Alec's mother had given the newlywed Elyse the very advice she had received from her mother. "In a new city, it is most important that you find acceptance. I recommend moderation in all things. The way you sit and the design of your chairs, the guest list for your dinner parties and the food you put on the plates. The secret to popularity is an inward generosity of thought, outwardly expressed in good manners. Sincerity, in my experience, is neither here nor there."

Alec supported his mother's views. Acceptance. Cleanliness can be purchased at the store, and as for Godliness, whatever it was, a position in the community certainly was no impediment. In Alec's business—it had something to do with money—acceptance came before all other virtues.

The Gardiners chose their friends, their charities, and their clubs accordingly. Alec suggested to Elyse that she swap her volunteer efforts on behalf of a particularly gruesome disease for a cause with an annual ball, where a gown would show her shoulders to advantage. And though she found the atmosphere close, Elyse complied.

Alec joined the City Club and the Rotary. After a few years, the Gardiners were invited to apply to the city's most prominent country club. The membership committee studied the nominating letters and soberly discussed the candidacy. The Gardiners were, all agreed, an attractive couple. High spirited, one member called Elyse, though not as a compliment. On the other hand, they were solid. Their fidelity to each other avoided the indelicacy that either might be sleeping with an existing member. That jump taken without barking a shin and their financial stability appearing sufficient, they were admitted.

• • •

Whatever it was that Alec did with money he did well. Aided by the wise associations he had chosen, his small firm prospered. Elyse gave birth to two children, and the Gardiners ripened to an attractive family. They ran through their days smoothly as if carried by the chassis of their fine German sedan. Elyse mingled among her peers. The traces of boredom, the endless conversations about skin peels and small hotels in Tuscany and the best grocer for arugula, those traces she shored up as one would spackle hairline cracks in plaster. Rumored to be a subscriber of the New York Times, Alec was otherwise considered steady. Two months after his fortieth birthday Alec was taken to lunch by two of the city's citizens, to ask whether he would be interested in the Grizzly Hackle.

The Grizzly Hackle was an enclave of twenty cabins on manicured shores of the best dry-fly water in the country. It lay in a remote valley five hours' drive from town. Members often arrived in small aircraft. Or large. Its roster, which included two ex-senators, a former Cabinet Secretary, and the presidents of a handful of major industrial companies, was considered the most exclusive in the region. Harold Parmenter, who had extended the invitation to Alec, told him the Gardiners would suit the Grizzly Hackle just fine and, with a wink, meant, Alec understood, to signal that he was lapsing into a foreign tongue, vice versa.

Alec was delighted. The Grizzly Hackle signaled the very peak of acceptance. The clients he would take there to fish would be instructed in his propriety, his probity, his success—the very characteristics he wished to suggest. The club operated informally though according to strict, century-old precedent. An impromptu character committee began its inquiries. They were inclined to be generous: they had a strong membership, but it was dying off at a rapid rate. Someone pointed out that Alec cared neither for bourbon nor for golf. Those deviations, coupled with his penchant for reading hardcover books, had given him a reputation as something of an intellectual. Still, the committee decided, those odd traits should not in themselves bar admission.

Elyse was a different matter. There had been those extraordinary incidents at the country club—two years in a row, the night of the hunter's moon, a watchman had seen a nude woman, running every fairway. One of the Hacklers mentioned that Elyse had her coloring. That was hardly, noted Harold Parmenter, a federal judge, admissible evidence. And another thing: a neighbor reported that Elyse had taken to shooting squirrels from her bedroom window with a pump-action twenty-two. The committee was inclined to be forgiving of small peccadilloes, particularly those connected with blood sport. The Gardiners' application was approved.

Alec studied furiously before his first weekend at the Grizzly. It was the annual stag, opening day. He arrived with texts and newly purchased gear, unpacked in one of the cabins on the long, tailored slopes leading down to the river, and angled diligently. He was a close reader, and while book learning alone did not make him a fisherman, he watched members in neighboring pools. By the end of the day he had caught his first trout. And at the dinner table that evening, when the conversation turned to investments, as it invariably did, he held his own.

He returned home flush with enthusiasm over his new hobby. He had managed to catch three fish, and had arranged two lunches with fellow Hacklers to discuss their equity portfolios. When he told Elyse about the weekend, his eyes shone.

"We must go. You'll love it."

"I don't like fish."

"That's not the point of it. No one keeps them. It's all catch and release."

"Why in the world would I want to catch them to let them go?"

Alec decided to change tack. Elyse would be an asset at table. Her dark beauty stopped every man, and her openness and her slightly, yes, he admitted to himself that was the word, Bohemian air usually captured their wives. He told her of the pastoral surroundings. The simple yet elegant cabins, log walls aged to a patina, the arts-and-crafts furniture inside, the plink and tinkle of ice buckets delivered at cocktail hour on the noiseless wheels of electric carts. The library of inscribed sporting books. In the dining hall, the great hearth decorated with famous fish caught by famous members, the shadow boxes of hand-wrapped flies with their entomological sources penned in calligraphy.

"It is," he said reverently, "a different era."

"I like this one," said Elyse.

4

But to please her husband, whom she loved, Elyse agreed to go. They set out by car, having no small aircraft, at least yet, on the weekend of October's first full moon. The air was chill clear and the aspen and cottonwood stood chrome yellow. On the trip down, confident that his wife would be respectful of the Grizzly's traditions, Alec asked her to read the considerable rules book.

"Does every fisherman," she wondered aloud, "get to bring a lawyer?" Alec smiled, and knew that her cynicism would melt away when she saw the beauty of the place.

• • •

And it did. The river that ran through the Grizzly's property spilled out of a fissured canyon. Its water moved from black to black-green to emerald through pools that had been planned to present every imaginable fly-rodding problem. Here and there the river was forded by footbridges, redwood planks with wire guards. The river's bed had been carefully groomed to make wading easy and to provide cover. A dirt road paralleled the five miles of stream, so elderly Hacklers could reach every pool. Strategic benches allowed the same fishermen to rest or indeed to fish long after their legs could not support them. Their only competition for the healthy rainbows that played in the surface was the occasional osprey or eagle that flew over. Elyse asked who had nominated the birds.

Alec helped his wife into a shallow pool and instructed her on the cast. She was a good athlete and soon was putting line where she wanted it. Confident of her success, he left her to her own.

And that is when the trouble started. Elyse made a dozen casts without result and became bored. So she reached into the aluminum foil wrap she'd stuck in her pocket and changed the lure. Soon she was netting sizeable fish, one after the other. So many, indeed, that one Conrad Muldoon, long-time member, stopped on the bank to watch her.

He had never seen anything like it. Five casts in a row, five fish. Five astonishing fish.

"My God," he finally called to her. "What are you using?"

Elyse smiled warmly and walked over to the shore. "Rumaki," she said.

"What?"

"Rumaki. It's an appetizer."

With this she hauled in the line and showed Conrad Muldoon, who happened to be the sergeant-at-arms for the Grizzly Hackle. There on the end of a bait-hook was a glob of stuff, vividly organic, and clearly neither fur nor feather.

"Madam, the rules establish that this is a fly-fishing stream."

"Not quite," said Elyse. "The rules say fly rods only. As you can see, I'm using a fly rod. They also say barbless hooks, and I've crimped the barb."

Conrad Muldoon was not accustomed to debate and rencounter. He retreated from the bank and directly sought out Judge Parmenter. A careful jurist, Harold Parmenter examined the buckram-bound rules of conduct. The list had served the enclave well: no radios, no cell phones, no helicopters, each member to tape his name to his whiskey bottle before placing it in the bar.

"Conrad, she happens to be right."

"Technically, I suppose. But fly rodding means flies only, isn't that a fair interpretation?"

Parmenter pursed his lips. "Fair, perhaps. But by no means exclusive. And I must tell you, by no means the more likely interpretation."

The weekend resolved itself. By sunset Elyse had taken a dozen fish, including several lunkers that no Hacklers had been able to tempt out of their lair. The management committee met—a handful of dedicated anglers wrote and enforced the rules— and adopted a clear prohibition against the use of bait, spoons, trolling devices, and spinning lures. Also natural or artificial food, whether for fish or human. They added those words since no one seemed sure of the ingredients for marshmallows. A letter announcing the rule went out over the signatures of Conrad Muldoon and Judge Parmenter, and they assumed that would be the end of it.

• • •

So, when one week later, his law clerk told Judge Parmenter that a young lawyer was on the line regarding the Grizzly Hackle, the judge never thought of Elyse Gardiner. He began to catalogue possible subjects. It might be the water rights issue, of course; the group wished to buy more, or perhaps the berm they intended to build along the county road, but not Elyse Gardiner.

"Judge Parmenter? I'm calling you in your capacity with the Grizzly Hackle Club. I've agreed to take Mrs. Gardiner's case."

"Case? What case?"

"This new rule. It constitutes ex post facto rulemaking. Mrs. Gardiner joined the Grizzly Hackle assuming that bait could be used."

"What are you talking about, young man? Mrs. Gardiner didn't join the Grizzly Hackle. Her husband did."

"Yes. But of course this is a community property state, so his dues were partly hers and his rights are similarly shared by her."

"She has no damages."

"She is not interested in money damages. This is a matter of principle. She enjoys fishing. Since she didn't catch anything on a fly, she wants to continue to use rumaki."

"What the devil is rumaki?"

"I believe, sir, it's chicken liver and water chestnuts wrapped in bacon." In the silence he added, "Usually seasoned with ginger and soy. Mrs. Gardiner left out the chestnut." More silence. "She tells me that cuts down the wind resistance."

"You cannot seriously consider litigating this issue?"

"Mrs. Gardiner is quite persuasive."

"Well that's dandy, young man. We'll see you in court. In fact, I hope to see you in my court."

"Oh, I don't think it will be your court, Judge. As a defendant, you would likely be disqualified to hear the case as well."

"What are you saying?"

"You, sir. In fact all the members of the Grizzly Hackle. It appears to be an unincorporated association. As you know the law treats that as a general partnership. I'm afraid we'll have to name all the Hacklers personally."

• • •

Harold Parmenter had the temperament of a good judge. He was patient and doggedly neutral, devoted to the seamless web that is American jurisprudence. He also had presided over enough settlement discussions to know that litigation, like war, results only when diplomacy fails; and that agreement is encouraged when each side appreciates the other's strengths.

He pressed for reason.

Muldoon, on the other hand, favored all-out battle. "Toss them both out on the seats of their waders."

But again the rules failed him: the grounds to discharge a member were repeated disorderliness (defined as three times in one year), non-payment of assessments, or drinking another Hackler's whiskey.

"If we try something high-handed," Parmenter warned, "we'll see a second lawsuit. Believe me. Unless we can reach a mediated deal, we will all be paraded in front of the court."

Harold Parmenter was, of course, the natural choice to negotiate. The young lawyer proved to be skillful and direct. He kept his client's goals in sight and assured the Judge that his purpose was not to inconvenience or embarrass the august Hacklers. He made no mention of the wishes of Alec Gardiner—for all the Judge could tell, Alec had no more control over his wife than the Judge.

A settlement was achieved. Elyse had found that she enjoyed fishing, especially when the catching was so lively, and she intended to keep at it. Out of sympathy for the Club's collective sensibilities, she would restrict her presence to one weekend a year. She accepted the validity of the new rule. In exchange for her concessions, during her weekend, the Club agreed to suspend that rule. And the fishing privileges of all non-Gardiner Hacklers.

• • •

So it is that every year, for two days beginning with the first full moon of autumn, the Grizzly Hackle closes. The hearth roars, the cocktail hour is subdued, and a single cabin shines with light. The five miles of stream are fished only by Gardiners—the children have become avid fisherfolk as well. And everyone catches fish.

And if one of those nights is cloudless, so that a pale disc of moon glims down on the rushing water, well past midnight there can be seen, were there eyes to see, over the manicured lawns and past the fishing benches and across the swing bridges that ford the riverdark foam, a racing figure, a racing female figure naked as a ghost.

LADY IN WADING

THE HOME POOL

The migrating color surprised her. Like those horrid lizards her brothers used to bring home every circus when she was a kid that would end up desiccated and dead under the radiator. But this was no chameleon, it was a shadow. Her father's cheekbones overhung the lower half of his face and, even now, in the north light of her studio, pitched a shadow. It made his cheeks move from a tallow color to something less healthy. She added brown ocher, dab by dab, to the viridian on the palette until she had it.

"You'll let me know when you want a break."

Her mother assured her this time. They would let her know. They spoke for each other without a glance. Forty-nine years of marriage span the margins, fuse differences of opinion.

Also differences of features? Had they grown to resemble each other, as people were said to do with their pets? Claire could not say. They looked a pair, the two of them. When you visualized one, the second appeared. Peel an onion and try to separate the outside of the skin from its inside.

She inspected her mother's eyes. What a luxury—to study your parents with this abandon. The blue was deceptive, more towards gray on close look. She fiddled on the palette, wrinkled her nose. Usually tone came quickly for her, but not now. Now, time's passing made her self-conscious, as if she were in a speaking contest and missing her lines. Don't keep them waiting. Move on to the sketch.

The painting was to be her gift for their anniversary. Claire's brothers were going to throw a party this summer at the cabin. All their friends, a country band—they liked the cowboy two-step—rum and tonics, blow-ups from their wedding album. Claire would present the portrait.

She sandpapered the charcoal stick to a finer point and began with those elusive eyes. They would be the Pole Star. She chalked in the lazy eyelid, the crow's feet, the tilt of the head. One of her mother's eyes, she noticed for the first time, was slightly larger. Perhaps not larger, simply more oval. Her thumb eased the faulty line into the grain and she sketched a second line over the smudge. The portrait, she had told them, would take two sittings. One for the palette and a sketch, a second for the faces in oil. She would commit later to the blue of the eyes, decide what to do about the stained look of her mother's hair. Would she include the liver spots? Her mother's brow was dappled as a spaniel. Include them all and it becomes a painting of spots.

Each session would be an hour at most, she had told them. She was facile with cartoons. Don't worry about likeness, get the shapes. Consider the gravitational forces. The charcoal made no sound but trembled in her fingers as it glided over the linen.

Now she pulled back from her shallow depth of field to the way people ordinarily observe. Their placid brows, the easy comfort of their bodies. Their eyes, unlike hers, relaxed and without focus. Their faces showed a mix of serenity and pride, as if they were at a first recital, watching her finish a sonatina. They saw her, she realized, as she was thirty years ago.

The charcoal continued its work. The brain might be else-where—often the best stuff happened when it was, when her eye connected directly to her hand.

Her mother was not tall, but she used to have the bearing of a tall woman. Now a deficiency of calcium rounded her shoulders and an excess gathered in ugly burls on the joints of her fingers. Would she paint those hands? One was curled within her husband's cupped grasp and the second rested without weight on his wrist. These hands had clothed her, held her from traffic, and pushed her into the world. Hooked her prom dress, unrolled her diplomas, and, in a ritual her mother never explained, gently slapped her before embracing her when she ran in breathless to report the first blood.

And more. These hands could manipulate a nine-foot cane rod to cast sixty feet of line. They were nowhere better suited to purpose. Claire smiled at the thought of her parents in the lurid twilight of the Home Pool, both straining beyond their full height to spot trout. He liked to fish the riffles above, she below. She could lay down line without a ripple, and so he ceded her the flat water. She would be inching tall, scouting for a telltale rise.

Concentrate on the gravitational forces. Get to how the subject stands in the world, dimension and authority. That's what painting was to Claire. Trying to set down, not the permanent—she wasn't that good—but what might be hard to get rid of. She positioned the arms and left the fingers indistinct.

"How are you both doing?"

"We're fine, dear." How was it possible to speak for another's lumbar muscles, another's bladder?

"And you, Dad?"

"Just as your mother says. Fine."

"Want a short break?"

"No, no," her father now the spokesman. "I'm enjoying myself."

Claire rose and stretched. Bent at the waist, put her palms to the floor and breathed. Her parents remained seated.

"Isn't that Schumann?"

"It is, Mother." Claire hadn't noticed the music. She had put it on for them.

"Didn't you play that piece?"

"No, Mother. I played Songs for Children."

"Is that Claire?" her father asked. "Is that Claire playing?"

"No Dad. It's Horowitz." She retook the stool and waited for their faces to lapse back into repose.

"You played that piece," her mother said. "I'm sure of it."

"Mom, that's Vladimir Horowitz. Chin up, please."

Her mother obliged. "I'm sure you're right," and she twitched her shoulders. "He plays well too."

Her father scolded them in a harsh whisper. "Claire's working."

She caught the bend of his head in a single line. He was over six feet but had lapsed into the habit of leaning over, a tree giving shade. Sometimes, when the cartoon went on easily, a line like that was as close as you got. The rest—the draftsmanship, the dead-on chromatics, the varnish that sealed in the time—and sometimes the life would go out of it. First came the idea. Then it was often a race to finish before the idea sank. The idea was fragile, lighter than air—it couldn't carry a lot of paint.

Again she drew her focus back: the line was so dead on it made her shiver. She tried to profile the face by blind contour, a single line done without lifting the charcoal or looking at the canvas. Then she studied his pupil. Get the eyes and you have a picture. Miss and you might as well quit. A dark ring surrounded the green flecks, a border that gave the eye—what? mutability? transience? The colors shifted as you watched. The lids, creased and thick, hung as if they were ready to drop and shut you out.

14

Suddenly Claire looked away. Something in her father's eyes compelled her to look down, and again at the stretched linen. She had not drawn them. Would she try? Sketch what she had seen? She looked again at her models—the specter had disappeared. Her father stared back with the same parietal contentment.

Did he know what passed in his eyes? If so he made no move to hide it. Where had it been? In the way the lid dragged across the arc of the pupil? In the blue-white corner? Perhaps it was her fear she had seen, not his.

She left the drawing unfinished. No face, no hands. She put down the angle of the shoulders, where the forearm crossed the thigh. Even cross-hatched in the old plaid shirt. That was a shirt he often wore on the stream, often with a box of wine cheroots in the breast pocket. Fishing was the only time he smoked them. Those vile things, her mother called them. Your father doesn't have to catch fish, she would say, he suffocates them. But Claire filled in no expression and decided not to render the eyes.

She looked at what she had. Studied her parents as if they were table objects in a still life: how the shapes charged each other, what the shapes held back. As a student she had sketched the Florence Pietà over and over. The teacher asked what she had learned, and she said, nothing.

"You studied the same piece for three weeks and you learned nothing? What holds it together?"

Love, Claire answered. It's held together by love.

She looked at the man and woman on the chairs before her, then at the easel, and she decided the sketch was no good. Inadequate. Whatever she could not address in their faces had dissipated and she saw the forms as lintel and post, stasis and change.

And it suddenly occurred to her the picture she would make.

"That's it," she said, rising. "You can stretch now. We're through."

They rose from their seats. Her mother stood unsurely on weakened knees, and he touched the top rung of the ladderback chair to straighten up.

"That was quite delightful," her mother said. "I enjoyed the Schumann."

"When will you want us again?" her father asked.

"I won't need you," Claire said. "I got so much today I won't need you again."

"You're sure? I quite enjoyed that, watching you work. Mother did too."

"I'm sure," Claire told them.

They walked out to the car. There was a short foot difference in their heights, and they formed an asymmetrical M, joining the letter by holding hands.

• • •

The party was wonderful. All their friends came, at least, as her father said several times, all the living ones. The cabin was an hour's drive on country roads so the consumption of rum and Champagne was moderate, but the food was plentiful and the toasts heartfelt.

It came time to open presents. Claire waited. She'd hoped the guests would leave, so her moment would be private. But people were curious and they stayed for the event and at last her mother was neatly undoing the neatly tied string. Unfolding the butcher paper, smoothing and folding it on its creases for a second use. Lifting away the tissue.

And holding up, tears in her eyes, her daughter's picture.

The light on the Home Pool was fading. Some might have thought the rose tint through the hay fields sentimental, but only those who had never fished that water in the golden light of a late June evening. In to her waist, she—and it was unmistakably she, even in waders and floppy hat, there was no mistaking—she held the rod over her head as a considerable fish bowed it to a crook. The fish had yet to break the surface. It must have sipped in the fly and sounded, for clouds, rosier still, reflected their perfect blooms in the water. Upstream, in the riffles, her husband had turned to watch. Hatless, the sleeves of his plaid shirt rolled to the elbow. His rod rested at his side. Between two fingers of the other hand there smoked the stub of a cheroot.

He turned to watch, and although the artist had lit the scene a grade too dimly to make out his expression, no viewer doubted it. It was a mix of serenity and implacable pride.

SOUTHPAW

UTE CREEK PASS

They drove south out of Cheyenne. He looked at a sky gray and heavy with unshed water and wished they weren't going.

"Could get rained on."

"Could happen," Craig said. Then later, "Sometimes it brings the fish up."

"Sometimes." He didn't think so, though. Sometimes it put the fish down. More often than not. One thing he knew: it would be cold and wet.

He would not have thought of going if Helen hadn't pushed him. Pushed him out the door. Do you good. Helen always knew what would do him good. Get out for the day. Remember how he used to love to go fishing with you?

He remembered. It was ages ago, when Craig was ten, eleven. Craig could fish all day. They would pack into the Wind Rivers, into the Medicine Bow Range, fish the Encampment, the North Platte. Craig wouldn't quit until it was too dark to see the fly. Lord, that was a long time ago.

"How far do you figure this place is, Dad?"

"Three and a half, maybe four hours. A long way to go for the day."

"We could stay over. I remember a motel in Hot Sulphur Springs." Craig had a road map spread across his knees, and his finger was tracing a route.

"Can't. Got to be at work tomorrow." He didn't mean it as a rebuke, although the words sounded harsh as they left his mouth. Craig had no work, no regular work. He got by. Just now he drove a truck for a firm in Tucson, when he wanted to. He and his girlfriend seemed not to need steady work to make a go of it, if you'd call the way they lived making a go of it. He wouldn't. No order, no regularity.

Can't live on nachos and love, he had told Helen, and she had said, Ed Berry, you old tree. Can't you remember what it was like?

Sure he could. He remembered he always liked clean sheets on the bed and fresh vegetables and knowing he was expected places. If that's what Helen meant, yes he could remember. If she meant being young meant being something else, no, he didn't remember that.

Why Craig was studying the map was a mystery. Ed knew the way well enough. Down into Colorado, where the fishing couldn't be as good as it was just twenty miles north of Cheyenne, then across the Divide and pick up the Colorado River at Granby. Seemed a long way to drive. Man Ed knew, more of a customer than a friend, had invited him down. Man leased out rights on his ranch to some oil fellows in Denver. Now with the spring he had the rights back, and kept telling Ed how it was great fishing. At least, sometimes. 'Course, he wasn't a fisherman himself.

Damn fool is probably wrong, thought Ed. Probably knows as little about fishing as he knows about balers. Man paid too damn much for every piece of equipment he had bought from Ed since they'd done business together.

"Sky may be opening up, Dad."

Sure enough, in the west a cleaved wedge of blue. Like someone took a slice out of a peach, to see if it was ready for eating.

"May be."

The drive was too long but easy. They had taken the Scout. Not that they needed it, but the whole idea of having a four-wheel drive was that it was Ed's car. For fishing and hunting. He liked that. He liked packing it with the gear, the long tubes for the fly rods, the hats—his old felt and Craig's, kind of a leather, hippie thing with a wide brim and a feather. Helen made sandwiches and stacked them, each neatly squared away in a plastic bag with the flap folded in and the sleeve pulled over, in an orderly column in the Igloo. Cans of diet pop for Ed, regular for Craig, chips, coleslaw, an apple each, and a nut bar.

They had risen before dawn and had taken a large breakfast. By the time he'd been driving an hour, thinking of what Helen had sent along, Ed was hungry.

"Reach back there, Craig, and get me an apple."

His son hooked a long arm over the rear seat and flipped open the cooler. He found an apple, took it from its little plastic bag and shined it on the whitened knee of his jeans. From deep in the pocket of his chamois shirt, he pulled out a knife and used his teeth to open its blade. Then he neatly halved the apple and with what seemed one motion removed the seeds and core.

He passed over the half to his father, offering it balanced on the tips of his fingers.

Ed felt better as he ate. Craig bit into the other half. Ain't that something, Ed thought. He's going to eat my half. Later on, if I want more apple, well, I'll have to eat his half. Isn't that an ass-backwards way of doing things, when we both start out with our own apple.

They were early for new growth. The trees showed the promise of bud but no buds, like a woman you know is pregnant and still flat-stomached, but ready. Now new green. Maybe south. Maybe there spring had come to peek through the colorless grasses, down in the

San Luis, where Ed used to go every autumn to shoot geese. The San Luis Valley, with its wide, glacier-forced floor, its marshes, its tiny streams that fed into the Arkansas, the Rio Grande, the Saguache. Ed loved that valley. 'Course, there was good bird country close to home. In the flyway of the Big Horn north of Sheridan, geese and duck were plentiful. No question, though, the country to the south was beautiful. If he didn't love it so, he would never drive the extra hours. Too far, too many people. Besides, he didn't like Coloradoans. Seemed as if every time he'd see one of their damn green license plates, it was where it wasn't supposed to be, hadn't asked permission, its driver had taken up in a hole he liked to fish. Too many of them. They've ruined their damned state, now they're going to ruin mine.

"Lord, what country."

Craig's words brought his eyes off the highway. It was true. They were coming across a high pass, over nine thousand feet. The snow-pack had not begun to melt, and you could see layers like a fancy pastry where each of the winter's snows had settled. Bleached, dormant fields stretched back from the snows to the peaks in the distance. Craig pulled out the thermos from the rear seat and poured two cups of coffee. Ed took his and breathed in its steam. The air smelled of sage and frost.

"Some country, huh, Dad."

His father nodded. "Some country," he said moments later.

"It's sure been great to get this week at home. Mollie and I have talked about getting you and Mom down to Tucson, but I told her, if I wanted to see you during bird season, I'd better make the trip down here."

"Not shooting so much any more."

"No? Why not?"

"Don't know," Ed said. "Doesn't seem as much fun anymore. Shot a lot of birds over the years. We have a locker full of dove and duck. Won't go hungry."

Craig laughed. "Really." Craig had this way of saying *really,* the way the kids do today, when they mean right, or I understand. Ed didn't like it.

There were reasons about the hunting, but he kept them to himself. It was true that the fun had gone out of it. For one thing, his hunting buddy had quit. Man was just sixty-five and he'd developed palsy. Or whatever they were calling it now. Didn't think he should be handling a loaded shotgun, shaking like someone in a home. Besides, Ed thought, I've tired of the blood. The feathers, the dead eyes, the blood. I've shot a lot of birds.

Craig let it go. He was on to something else. What color he and Mollie painted the walls and where they wanted to go this summer and whether you were better off with a gas range or electric. Craig never lacked for talk.

They rolled through Granby. At the far end of town they stopped for gas and bought single-day licenses at a shanty store that sold T-shirts, salmon eggs, and homemade jerky by the register. Back on the road, they picked up the Colorado River as it ran west. From here it flowed across the state, through Glenwood Springs and down through dams and canyons into the Sea of Cortez. All that water dumping into a Mexican ocean and ranchers in Wyoming thirsting for it.

It was close to eleven when they found the turnoff past Parshall. Craig jumped out to open the wire gate and got back in after the car rolled over the cattle guard. A jeep road, rutted and splotched with cow pies, jogged down to a grove of cottonwoods. Ed steered the Scout in among them and turned off the motor.

"Raining," he said. First rain of the season. Wash out the old.

"Not too bad. A drizzle."

Craig was right. They got out and put on their waders, rain jackets, vests. Hard by them, beyond the grove of trees, ran the river, black as rock.

"No hatch on."

"None yet," Craig said. "How 'bout we eat now? Then we can fish straight through?"

They sat in the light rain, he on the car fender, Craig cross-legged on the damp ground, on its blanket of leaves and dust. They set the cooler between them and put their pop cans on it. Ed watched the river and saw nothing. On the opposite bank, an ouzel hopped about on the rocks searching for bugs.

They decided to split up. Ed walked downstream and Craig up. They were to meet at the car at four if they didn't see each other before.

At first he fished hard. There were no hatches and no fish fed on the surface. And so he fished deeper, drifting a nymph, then a wet fly to find deep-lying trout, free-drifting the fly as if it had just jarred loose from its pupal shuck attached to the riverbed stones. People put nymphing down—the dry-fly purists put it down—but it took skill, intuition. You had to feel that fish mouth the nymph, sense when the line veered or stopped for the briefest moment, and strike before the fish spit out the tiny lure. It was a skill, and lots of people fished for years before they picked it up and lots more never got it at all.

So he concentrated and fished hard, but in three hours he found only two fish, both browns, spotted red and silver with golden bellies shining in the faint March light. It was as if the fish, not the sky, were the source of the light. After he netted each fish, he slipped out the hook, righted the trout in the water and let it go. The fish swam off slowly, without fear, and swam out of his sight and out of the memory of the encounter. By the time it disappeared under the stream's elodea beds each was again a wild thing.

Now he had waded upstream to where the car was parked. He was chilled from the river and the constant mist. He took off his waders and vest, got in the driver's door, and turned on the heater. He leaned back and lowered the headrest so it bolstered the base of his skull. The warm air blew through the fan belt and he could feel the dampness melt from his leggings and his wool shirt.

He woke. He reached briefly, urgently, for his dream—it was an important one—but he couldn't bring it back. Where had he been? Had he been younger? Stronger? It would not return.

Again he put on the clothes of his pursuit. Now he walked upstream, to see what new riffles and pools the river held.

The rain had stopped and the clouds seemed to have come together. They made distinct forms now, hanging lower and bellied with rain. Rays of the sun bounced among the forms, and while he sensed light through the seams of the clouds, there were no shadows.

Peering around an oxbow, beyond the willows, he saw his son. Craig stood erect in midstream, the river low about his thighs, watching his fly line as an osprey will watch a feeding fish: when it falters, when it hesitates, he moves. The fly went through its perfect drift, and Craig rolled out line with a swift push of his rod, into an elegant serpentine above his head, and allowed another cast to float onto the water's surface.

Thinking like a fish isn't enough, he had taught him. You have to be that river bed and those stones and that mayfly nymph, sweeping down in the current. You have to see that trout pick you out, leave his feeding station, slowly sip you in. Then you strike.

Ed watched the boy for an hour. Craig caught several fish. Some good size. Each one he played from the reel with a look in his eye that Ed recognized.

Cannot believe he'd want to leave Cheyenne, Ed thought. Much as he loves this country. Good a fisherman as he is. He remembered the arguments about Craig's quitting high school. How he didn't want to work in Ed's office or out back, in the yard. You'd think most kids would love that job, driving tractors and backhoes and doing stuff that most kids dream about doing. Some things, Ed thought, I just won't understand. Helen had said, You got to let him go, so he let him go. And now what he had was a kid who lived in Arizona, who could fish like that, and nothing to show for the years but wonderment about what he hadn't done right.

25

They agreed that the clouds looked ominous and that, with the low flicker of lightning beyond the rim of the land, they ought to move along. Craig had the map out as Ed stowed the last of the gear into the boot of the wagon.

"Look here, Dad. See that road? Looks like it can save us time."

Craig was right. A dirt road, bearing a state highway number, cut a diagonal across the perpendicular route they had used that morning.

"Don't know. Might be a jeep road."

"I don't think so, Dad. I mean, it's a state highway, and here on the key they list jeep roads dotted, not solid. Looks driveable. Ute Creek Pass. What say? Want to try it?"

"Could just as soon cost us time as make it up."

"Could. Still, we're in no rush, and it's a new way to go. Let's give it a try. I'll drive, if you want."

Ed glanced at the gathering dark. Beams of sun snuck through the clouds like reef fish and swam to earth. What the hell, he thought. That's what the Scout is for.

He handed Craig the keys. "Let's give it a try."

The turn was well marked by a sign.

UTE CREEK PASS

SUMMIT 19 MILES

Ed figured if they did even half the speed on the pass, they'd cut some time off the return trip. Nineteen miles to the summit, another fifteen miles down. He didn't want to be on that road when they lost the last glow of dusk. Funny feeling to have your kid drive you. Ed had never been a passenger in the Scout.

The road snaked up a long, easy rise. After five miles, the pavement stopped, and they were on gravel. Then the gravel gave out, and it was bladed dirt, red and hard packed, the marl slick under the headlights of the climbing Scout. No cars, no signs, no evidence that the road led anywhere but into the balconies of heaven.

They hadn't spoken since the turnoff. Ed began to wonder if this was such a good idea. A breakdown, for instance. You could slide off the road and snap a connecting rod, and who the hell was there to help them? At the point of no return, a three-hour walk back to nowhere. This was a damn foolhardy idea, and he was angry that he'd let himself be talked into it.

They climbed, passing patches of ponderosa. Through the trees was cut an occasional timbering path, and the trails made Ed brighten that perhaps all civilization was not behind them. The evening light came across the land low and bright, like a filtered spotlight. In the rays of one of those lights, Ed saw a sign by the roadside.

UTE CREEK PASS SUMMIT 6 MI.

TABERNASH MINE 6 MI.

"Did you see that, Dad?" Craig sounded relieved. Ed took some comfort that Craig too was rethinking the route they had chosen. "Did you see that? What do you suppose they're mining up here?"

"Don't know," said Ed. "I never heard of no mining up here."

Both men now leaned forward in the car. Craig pushed the speed a little, drifting around one curve on the wet dirt and sending a chill to Ed's groin. The sky was backlit, the last band of light only now being forced out of existence by the clouds of settling rain.

The engine labored at the higher altitudes. They had come up several thousand feet from the river. Not as high as the route over, still the car seemed to rear and pitch. Every time it slipped down a gear the car lurched, and with every lurch Ed swore to himself it would be the last automatic transmission he'd buy. Fine for a woman's car, but if he was going to have a mountain car, damn it, it would have a standard shift. This was a three-legged horse.

They came around another serpentine turn, rod cases rolling noisily in the back, and there at the head of a moraine stood the damnedest sight Ed had ever seen. In the middle of nowhere, at the top of a Colorado mountain pass, a four-story building with three giant stacks coming out of it. Surrounding the building was a hurricane fence twelve feet high, all lit up as if it were a ball field for a night game. The mill was set in the hollow of a mountain peak that had been scooped out like a cantaloupe. What was missing wasn't fruit, but rock blasted free and rolled and crushed for extraction. On either side of the building were long, rectangular settling ponds, dammed and still, each the size of a football field, each shimmering green and electric as a tourmaline.

"My God," said Craig.

Ed said nothing. They drove the few hundred yards to the plant's main gate. The road passed right by it. Craig braked the car to a halt and looked out.

"What in hell do you suppose it is?"

"Right there," said Ed. There was a metal sign on the gate with black lettering.

TABERNASH MINE AND MILL

UTE CREEK PASS

INTERNATIONAL METALS CORP.

NO TRESPASSING

Ed had rolled down his window to get a better look. A voice split across the loudspeaker and startled them both.

"Help you fellows?"

They peered in. Behind the gate, under the only overhead light that was not trained on the plant, stood a man in a yellow hard hat. In his hand he held a microphone the size of a grenade. It hooked up to a black conical speaker mounted on the top of the gate.

"No. Just looking."

"Fine." He turned to walk away.

"Ask him what they mine, Dad."

"Don't be a damn fool, Craig. None of our business."

"Go ahead. Ask him."

Ed swallowed. "Say . . ."

The man turned.

"What do you all mine here?"

"Molybdenum."

"That right?" Ed said. He turned to Craig. "Molybdenum."

"Damn," said Craig.

Ed rolled up his window and, as if in concert, they looked forward and Craig drove away. The trip down the east side of the pass was uneventful.

"Molybdenum," said Craig as they rejoined the paved highway. "What the hell is molybdenum?"

"Use it for steel. Use it in the making of steel."

"That place, Dad. It looked like it could have been in Russia or somewhere. Know what I mean?"

"I do," said Ed. "It could have been in the Himalayas or someplace like that."

"Really. Coming on that in the middle of nowhere and all. Wasn't that something?"

Ed agreed that it was something. He didn't speak any words, but he nodded and in the darkness Craig knew he had.

They descended the pass, saying little. The sequence of road surfaces was reversed—the bladed dirt road, then gravel, then pavement and they knew they were close to the highway. At the spot where the two roads again joined, there was a convenience store with two gas pumps.

"You going to feel like eating before we get home?" Ed asked.

"Whatever you like. Maybe we can grab something for the car."

They parked and went into the store. It was empty except for the woman behind the counter. She was reading *Screenplay*. In front of her a small portable black-and-white television set with an enormous aerial was broadcasting a game show.

"Howdy," said Ed.

"Evening."

"Cold," said Craig, rubbing his hands.

"Not yet," she said and smiled. She was Ed's age, maybe older, a big woman with bushy gray hair. She wore a heavy ribbed cardigan sweater over a flannel shirt and jeans.

"Got anything hot to eat?"

"I can heat you up some sandwiches," she said. "In the nuker. And there's coffee."

Ed looked at Craig.

"Sounds just right," he said.

They returned to the Scout with a paper bag full of food and a six-pack of Coors. Ed drove, while Craig handed him his dinner. He took a can of beer and propped it between his thighs, and with his left hand on the wheel took what Craig offered. They ate chili dogs, and potato chips, and French fries in a cardboard dish shaped like the boats Ed used to make from newspaper for Craig and the girls when they were kids. It rained heavily as they ate, but they had dried off from the stream and the Scout's heater hummed under the dash.

"Dad?"

"Um?"

"Mind if I ask you something?"

"No. 'Course not."

"Why'd you and Mom get married? I mean, how did you decide you wanted to?"

"Well," Ed said. He licked salt from his fingertips.

"Well, the usual reasons. You know."

Craig was silent, and Ed thought a minute.

"I mean, we loved each other and wanted to be together. And of course it wasn't like now. You didn't live together."

"Did you have girlfriends before Mom?"

Ed smiled. "Yeah. Sure. I mean, one or two serious ones."

"Ones that you slept with?"

"Yeah. That too. Sex was around then, too." Ed smiled, and he looked over to see Craig.

"I just mean, how do you know you want to marry one and not the other?"

Ed let some highway go by.

"You thinking of getting married?"

"No," Craig said quickly. "But you know, Mollie and I talk about it and all. You know how women are."

"Sure. I guess we did too. Well, your mother and I kind of lived together, but not in the open. And if you wanted to have kids and everything, well, we thought we ought to get married."

A semi hauling two trailers of cattle came at them. Through the tires Ed felt the rumbling of the truck as it passed and as it moved away from them. Rain streaked the windshield and the night surrounded them.

"Did you want to have kids?"

"Can't say as how I'd really thought it through. Your mother did, and it sounded OK to me." He drank the last sip of beer, turned warm from the heat of his body, and handed Craig the empty can.

"Another?"

"Not yet. Don't want to make a piss stop in this weather."

They rode for a while in the quiet.

"Well, what do you think of it?" Craig asked.

"Of what?"

"Marriage."

Ed took a breath. He hadn't thought of it, at least not for a while.

"Well. It's been different."

"What do you mean?"

"Different from what I thought. I guess I thought it'd be like having your best friend sleep over all the time. But it's been different. More complicated."

"How so?"

"With kids and all. Don't get me wrong. We wanted all you kids, you and your sisters. But it sure takes energy. I don't suppose I knew anything about it. It just changes your life, and you don't know it's coming."

Craig seemed to ponder that. Ed wasn't satisfied with it, but it was all he could think to say.

"We got cinnamon twists and jelly doughnuts."

"A twist," said Ed. "And another beer. Can't eat jelly doughnuts while you steer."

31

"Want me to drive?"

"Nah. We're an hour out. No more."

Ed ate the pastry. It left his hands sticky, and he gathered the dew from the fresh can of beer to wash them. They would be out of the mountains soon and he could pick up Cheyenne on the radio.

"Damn," said Craig.

"What's that?"

"Sex sure is a strong thing."

Ed nodded. "Sure is."

The road passed into a flat part, and they moved faster across the open range. There was an occasional car now, and with each one that crossed there was a flick of bright lights and the empty wake of air as they crossed.

Now the rain came mixed with snow against the windshield, hard to tell apart, and Ed edged the heater up a notch. As it grew colder, the snow might start to stick, and the driving would get tricky. But if that happened, he didn't notice. Soon they were out of the hills, the flakes and raindrops fighting for equilibrium, and he was turning north toward home.

• • •

The next morning he was surprised to hear voices in the kitchen. Craig hadn't been up for breakfast since he'd arrived. He had noticed— it rankled him to leave for work every morning while his son slept through and his wife waited to fix another breakfast. But this morning, as he stood shaving in the bathroom at the top of the stairs, he heard the voices of Helen and Craig in the kitchen. He hurried to join them.

"You'd have to see it," Craig was saying. "It was like a sci-fi movie or something. Wasn't it, Dad?"

"What's that, Craig?"

"The mine. The Tabernash Mine."

"Yeah. It was something to see."

"I guess," Craig agreed. "Like another planet. Out in the middle of nowhere, Ma. A sci-fi movie."

"That must have been something to see," said Helen. "How come you didn't mention it?"

Ed shrugged. He poured himself a cup of coffee from the Pyrex pot and sat down at the kitchen table. Helen put a glass of juice and a plate with bacon and two slices of toast in front of him.

"I asked your father about the trip."' Helen spoke as if to Craig. "You want to know what he said?"

"What?" Craig and Helen were looking at each other in complicity, getting ready to laugh.

"Not many fish." They laughed and Helen repeated what Ed had said.

"That's true," said Ed. "Not many fish."

"It was a good trip, though," Craig said.

Ed looked at him and nodded. He chewed his toast slowly. When he had finished and had drunk his coffee, he looked at his watch.

"Damn. The time. Got to go." He rose and left in a rush, although it was the time he always left for work, even a little early.

SOLACE

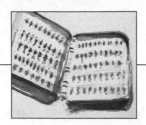

THE VIEW FROM BUFFALO MOUNTAIN

How did it happen that Rocky Kansas Campaneris owned a shack on that piece of land?

Rocky's grandfather was a Basque who shot a man, or thought he did, and left his village by way of Marseilles to come to the United States. Once here he traveled west in search of familiar landscape. For a time he herded sheep near Bozeman, Montana, but mostly he worked the coal mines. Rocky's father worked the open pits of Butte and the placers of Colorado. Underground, too. Gold and silver in the loop north of Creede and molybdenum on top of John C. Fremont Pass.

He was running a slurry in the New Mexico coal fields when he met his wife, cooking and making beds, and she looked as if she might have blood from his grandfather's country. That was the five-eighths Tesuque. The other fractions she kept secret, like the last ingredient of a family recipe.

They named their children after American heroes. Rogers Hornsby Campaneris was a hard drinker, drove his truck off a bridge and drowned in the Ruby River, just when the water was starting to

35

run clear and the fishing was picking up. Gasoline from the tank killed trout three miles downstream. Babe Didrikson Campaneris married five times and, the last Rocky had heard, was a glazier in Ventura, California where she'd been lured by a promise of no snow.

Rocky K was born with a short left leg. He was named after a lightweight fighter who held the world championship for almost a year. His father was at the Pocatello Civic Auditorium the night Rocky Kansas fought three men, though not all at once. At twelve, Rocky K quit school and took a job pumping gas. With a limp the only thing going for him, he had decided to find the work that no one else wanted.

Early in his twenties he wandered into the office of Summit Mining and Metals in Climax, Colorado, and got a job underground. He apprenticed on an air drill, down 8,000 feet where the pressure was so great the rock walls were hot to the touch. He handled machines—an overshot loader and a slusher hoist—and got himself promoted. Until the accident, he was a powder man making good money. But a blasting cap went off early and he lost three fingers and part of the meat of his left hand.

The union got him permanent disability, but he figured, hell, he'd rather work, so he went back under as a timber man. Those are the souls first in the hole after it's blown, to shore it up. Because of the risk that the rock might run they get good pay, almost a dollar an hour more than the ordinary miner.

So Rocky spent twenty years pulling tin and tungsten and gold out of the hills of central Colorado. But the tin gave out and when the price of steel went south, no one wanted tungsten. The company shut down the mine. He had a pension and they had to pay him anyway, so they shipped him to their zinc deposits on Colorado's Buffalo Mountain in the San Cristobal Range. It was an old mine, silver in its heyday. Rich ore then, but since the Forties these claims were spare. In their midst lay the little shanty town of Cimarron City, and that of course is right smack where this story is headed, for everyone has

heard of the skiing at Cimarron City, the Mozart concerts, the confer-
ences on world peace, and the high-grade cocaine.

They planted Rocky K in a rooming house on the outskirts of
Cimarron City and he worked forty-four hour weeks—half-day Saturday—running the cage. The hills are honeycomb around there, and
if you know your way and don't get thirsty or smart, they say you can
walk from Cimarron City all the way to Crested Butte and never see
the sky. Rocky worked his hours and on his free time trapped, fished,
drank whiskey with ginger ale, and took his comfort with Doris
Quinton in her three-room apartment over the Yankee Clipper Diner.
Doris owned the Diner, and she was as ugly as a skillet full of chicken
livers but nice as can be to Rocky K.

And then one April, thirty years ago, a visitor passing through
stood on Buffalo Mountain and looked across the glaciated valley and
saw what's been there since October, what's been there every year—
snow. Marshmallow piles of it, long, white couloirs of it, dangling off
Cimarron Peak like the braided hair of a woman. The north face of
the mountain tucked under so that snow held long into the spring
when all the other hills around had poked through brown and forsak-
ing of winter. The mountain stretched back to the horizon and
descended at different angles, angles that to this visitor's eye were
named Beginner, Intermediate, and Expert.

Commerce brought change: forest service permits, industrial rev-
enue bonds, architectural committees, logos, designers, and magazine
photographers. Soon an acre lot on Buffalo Mountain cost four mil-
lion plus or minus, houses in town went for a thousand a foot, and
Summit Mining had been paid more than a year's earnings to close
down its small and unprofitable operation.

Close down, but not sell out. Summit agreed with the Ski Corpo-
ration to discontinue mining activities for fifty years, to suspend its
surface easements, and to seal off the portals of about a dozen shafts
that might otherwise ensnare the tourists coming to enjoy, as the
brochure says, the outdoor experience.

To preserve its mining claims, Summit was required by law to log fifty man-hours of work annually on each site and stand ready to prove it. The price of minerals flutters and dives like a tailless kite in a high wind, and every miner knows the stories of holding on, whether it's a major company or a lone prospector, holding on until the rock recovers fabulous values. Summit was no different. Having dismissed its crews and sold its boarding houses for development, they determined to keep a staff of one. Rocky Kansas Campaneris knew all the properties, he could operate every piece of equipment, he could even handle and store explosives. Besides, he was pensioned, work or no.

They cut him a deal. As long as he wanted, he could stay in Cimarron City. He was to gather the tools and equipment and write up an inventory. Then he was to perform the annual claim work, rotating around and packing into each site, to make sure the land was posted, its adit sealed tight—no sign of vandals and no danger to hikers.

For all that, they agreed to keep him at a timber man's pay. And they would give him outright the equipment shed. It wasn't winterized and it had no plumbing, but electricity and water were hooked up. The deal was fine with Rocky K. The pay was generous, even in a town where the price of groceries would soon triple, but at the time it was more than he could spend. As for the shack, he'd fix it up. He was good, he used to say, with his hand.

So Rocky K, who had spent most days of his adult life underground, came out into the sun, bandy-legged, gimpy, and happy as a butterfly. And that is how he came, in his sixtieth year, to own this shed, silver packets of insulation tacked to its outside and blankets of tar paper on its roof to keep in the heat, but his own shed, the only space he had ever had to himself.

It must be said of the neighboring plutocrats that they enjoyed this presence in their midst. They contemplated their ghetto of excess, where mansions were built in every architectural style from Loire Valley chateau to Bauhaus, all perched on the mountainside like turkey buzzards, their hot tubs steaming in winter and in summer their

38

stereos singing to each other across pool and tennis court, and enjoyed the site of the shack. Rocky K was part of the Old West. Better still if he would live in a log cabin, like those quaint ruins on the pass where thousands of imported Chinese laborers had been billeted while they built the first railroad grade across the San Cristobals. That would be more appropriate, more ecological. One or two neighbors even suggested the idea to Rocky, that he put logs around the shack, get into the Cimarron City Spirit. Rocky politely declined, saying, No thanks. And when pressed for a reason, Ain't interested.

Money and people changed the valley. Almost everyone, particularly those who had made the changes, deplored them. The town wasn't what it used to be. Rich Midwesterners didn't like the way rich New Yorkers spent their money. Rich New Yorkers resented the Mexicans, Mexicans the gaudy folk from Beverly Hills, and everyone spoke ill of the Texans.

Rocky K didn't pay too much mind. He didn't call the new people new people, or crassholes, which was the locals' name for them. He did notice that it grew more difficult to trap, for badger and fox were scurrying to quieter ground. But he found a way to offset the few dollars he had made from bootleg pelts. Every winter he would throw a tow chain, a shovel, and a block and tackle into the back of the company pickup and pull sport utility vehicles out of the drainage ditch that bordered the steep and twisting road up Buffalo Mountain. That work melted away when the ski season ended, but come summer the same drivers would run their four wheelers into irrigation ditches, so he towed and changed tires and replaced broken connecting rods. And for recreation there were fish. While the hunting had suffered, there were always fish. The newcomers waded the river by the roads. But they neither walked nor broke the law, so if you were willing to hike a ways and cross barbed wire, why, you'd find your limit.

Rocky's life changed in little ways, too. These folks were mightily fond of waving. Rocky waved back and went his way, paying the changes little mind and the new folks less.

Not Doris. People told her all this prosperity would be a boon to the Yankee Clipper, but her business was off. Hard to find help when no waitress or cook could afford to live within forty miles of Cimarron City. It was a puzzle to Rocky that these new people didn't like her cooking. When customers came in to study the menu, you could see their noses work. Some would leave right off, others when they found they couldn't get a drink or a glass of wine, although why they confused eating and drinking Doris didn't understand. Those who stayed tended to pick at their food. The chicken fried steaks came back half-eaten, the chili pecked over. Business folks had tried to buy out her lease, but she wouldn't have it, and so long as she wouldn't, Rocky K was living happy.

Given its surroundings Buffalo Mountain itself was unimposing. At just under 10,000 feet it faced dead into the highest peaks of the San Cristobal range. Its significance to modern Cimarron City was not its geology or prominence, but its view. A single road wound up its bare southern side. From anywhere on that road or the lots it served you could see the ski area. You could watch skiers shooting out of the groves of aspen and Engleman spruce. You could look off your sundeck to compute the wait for the lift. All the while, the sun in the southern sky shone on your property, warming it, getting its heat captured in elaborate solar storage batteries that folk particularly favored for vacation homes. No matter that they were the very folk who consumed draughts of fossil fuel arriving in Gulfstreams. The ski hill was ringed by massifs. It was the newest geologic formation in the Rockies; its mountains stood rugged and sharp, yet to be beaten down by the wind. And every day of the year, if you were so privileged, you could watch the sun cross those spires and set behind them, watch the stars glisten like sprinkles on a birthday cake. It was a cake, it was a feast. And there were a limited number of slices.

Lew Sheldon bought himself a serving. Lew had inherited his father's small department store. Never a source of wealth, the store had suffered under haphazard management and price pressures. Competition had left Lew with an increasingly large overstock. In what he was sure were his last days of solvency, he opened an outlet store in the wrong part of town, named it The Dust Bin, and stocked it with his considerable supply of unsalable merchandise.

The results were astonishing. In a few years, Dust Bins, flashing their distinctive magenta and gold logos, popped up in suburban malls. Lew had a deft touch—his ads and window displays showed clothes bought by the container and destined for third-world countries. Lew had not changed—taste had. A generation of teens decided to dress as if they were on soup lines. Lew soon had over five hundred stores and a listing on NASDAQ. Money poured in.

That kind of money needs a home. Actually, several homes. Sheldon had not inherited or yet cultivated a rich man's hobbies. The only collectible that appealed to him over the years was houses. Four he had designed himself, and each had a special meaning to him. His first in Bridgehampton was still his favorite. The beach house in Montenegro Bay had been a wedding present to his second wife, or so she told the court. The fishing lodge in Sitka he had visited only twice, but he'd landed a salmon each time. He sold the villa and lands in Valle de Bravo when the air got so bad you couldn't see to drive out of the Mexico City airport. Now he wanted somewhere new for his winters. His new wife wanted to try skiing. Where better than Cimarron City?

He assembled his architects in the Dust Bin headquarters on Seventh Avenue. The first decision, they told him, was site. From that all else would follow.

The team was organized. A Cimarron City broker quickly found a magnificent location, a long, alpine bench with artesian springs at its low end, views of the San Cristobals at 200 degrees, easy access. It was zoned for three residential sites, twenty-four acres in all, but you could pick up all three. Sheldon did. There were a few shortcomings, but they could be fixed. Only willow and scrub grew in the thin soil of the mountain. He would have to move a lot of earth to plant what he had in mind. A utility line ran smack through the middle of the property, but it could be buried when they laid the fiber-optics cable. Finally, on the far side of the road, smack in center foreground of his mountain view, sat an unsightly equipment shack. Solution: buy it and tear it down.

Work crews began as soon as the snows cleared. They excavated the site and laid the foundation. The high country has a short building season and Mr. Sheldon had announced this project would be brought in on time. Every carpenter, mason, tinsmith in the valley benefited; every electrician, landscaper, tile man, and grouter. Mornings at seven, the roar of generators and the patter of hammers tripped down the mountain. The noise roused tourists who had come for a week's quiet.

It didn't bother Rocky. He was up at five, out of that unsightly shack and at the Clipper by half past, eggs, bacon, coffee, home fries and a smoke, maybe on cold days a piece of apple pie, and he was bouncing along back roads on the way to one of Summit's claims before the first nails of the morning were pounded.

It didn't bother Rocky when they had to turn off his water to run the lines for the swimming pools and the Jacuzzis, master and guest; when two front-end loaders blocked his driveway for a week while they dug the canals for the stream bed; when the hatchery dumped fingerlings on three different occasions and they came up dead and putrid in the August morning because the pump didn't deliver enough oxygen, they'd need more power; or when the moving trucks used his driveway to off-load the Aubusson carpets, the Jenn-Air ranges, the commercial meat lockers and refrigerators, the Bechstein concert grand that no one played, the Queen Anne cherry block front desk-on-frame, and the Federal inlaid mahogany tall case clock, estimated as early 19th Century.

Rocky simply paid no mind.

He paid no mind to the building itself, its thirty thousand feet perched on the hill across the road, a glass and steel raptor ready to swoop. The house spread in layers over the hillside, a second story cantilevered out over space and the topmost story, master bedroom suite, plopped as a cornice to hold down the house. Rocky K would roll out of bed, sprinkle salt on his finger and run it over his teeth, slip on jeans and a shirt, and sneak out into the rising morning. There the monster building would be, angrily reflecting the first sun's rays in his eyes. He'd squint, pull open the door of the Ford pickup, pea green except for the gray primer of the right rear fender that he meant someday to paint, and go about his business. On weekends, that reflection shone in and woke him before he was ready. He had never needed curtains in his shack, but the glare was a nuisance. He found several empty cement sacks and nailed them over the windows so weekends he could sleep in.

It seemed that Cimarron City's newest architectural marvel was accepted by all. Many of the mountain's residents buzzed in their twenty thousand square-feet about profligacy, ostentation, and whatever element it was they perceived that Sheldon represented, but did no more. Sheldon was, after all, what Cimarron City property was for, it was why people talked of the Spirit of Cimarron City, why they trademarked the term: that particularly robust combination of culture, sport, and indulgence.

All seemed peaceful. Until the arrival, the advent, fourteen days before Christmas, of Mr. and Mrs. Lew Sheldon.

Shawn, his bride of six months, was thrilled with the house. Lew had arranged that the car from the airport drop them at the base of Buffalo Mountain. There they were met by a horse-drawn sleigh, complete with an authentic bell collar that Lew's shopper had found in Vermont. They reached the rose marble steps that led to the entrance of the house. Shawn stood aside as Lew threw open the fifteen-foot carved doors from Umbria. There in the entry hall stood a two-story blue spruce, decorated and lit, presents at its base in perfect disarray, as though this were a catalogue tree, and its fruit had freshly fallen. Shawn—she had kept her modeling name—thought Lew the most romantic man with the most generous spirit, and indeed he was.

While the help unpacked for them, they dined on red wine and oyster pie. And then to bed in their aerie, the curtains drawn back to see the sparkling of a December night in the Rockies.

In the morning, Lew brought her to the window to look down upon the old town of Cimarron City, to attend the majesty of the granite peaks stretching in private panorama from one end of his property to the other, to admire the blanket of new snow fallen in the privacy of the night, white as the finest feathers.

And there, in the cross hairs of his view, was the shack of Rocky Kansas Campaneris.

Lew sent Shawn ahead to the lifts and canceled his ski plans. He summoned his lawyer, his accountant, the New York architect, the Denver architect, and the local real estate broker to a conference call. There was quick consensus. The shack had slipped through the cracks. We asked Campaneris about selling, the broker explained, but he'd been vague. Not exactly vague, it's just that he wasn't a seller.

At some price, needled Lew, at some price everyone's a seller.

Best way to handle this was directly. Lew struggled into new Caribou boots, donned his parka, and crossed the road. He found his way through the oil drums in the yard, ignored the cans of antifreeze and machine lube stacked against the side of the shack. Took off a down-filled glove and knocked on the door.

It was Sunday. Rocky K was home.

"Hello," said Lew. "My name is Lew Sheldon. I live in that house." He pointed over his shoulder without looking. Rocky squinted and said nothing.

"Mind if I come in?"

Rocky stepped aside. This was his first visitor.

If Lew was unsure about the need to take action—which he wasn't—his visit increased his resolve. The shed was a single room. In its center, without so much as a wall or curtain, hooked on to pipes that rose naked from the concrete floor, stood a stove, a refrigerator, a toilet bowl, and a bathtub. Around the outskirts of the space, some rudimentary furniture, cases of canned goods, some opened on the floor, others stacked, a disassembled electric motor, a bed, and several pieces of machinery (each the size of a small dog) that he couldn't name. Two shotguns and a fly rod leaned against one wall, and by them in a corner lay several leg traps, though Lew wasn't sure about those either.

"Mr. Campaneris, let me come right to the point. I'd like to buy your land."

"No thanks," said Rocky K. "Ain't interested." His father had told him that you could say No thanks with pride. It was only when you started saying Yes please that you were in trouble.

"But you haven't heard my price yet."

Rocky nodded. "That's so."

"Price," Lew put on a winning smile, "is important."

Rocky said nothing. He saw no reason to argue.

"Everything has its price. You've heard that old saying?"

"Nope."

"Mr. Campaneris, you're a shrewd cupcake. You figure you're entitled to top dollar. I respect you for it. Let's do it this way. You tell me your price."

"Don't have none. Ain't interested."

Lew looked at him a long moment. "Well," he said, clapping his hands together and looking around. "This is homey." He walked in a tight circle, stepping over a twelve-inch flywheel.

"I see you're a fisherman. I'm taking that up. Going to take lessons, right here." Lew walked over to the long wooden table and noticed the vice.

"What's that?"

Rocky shrugged. "For tyin'."

"Flies?" Rocky nodded again.

"Think of that. You tie your own flies. Those feathers and, what is that stuff?"

"Muskrat."

45

Lew looked at him. It couldn't be this hard. Perhaps he would put Rocky in an ad. Sitting in front of the vice, a long pelt of muskrat. Lew's ads had made Depression styles hot. Was there a way to corner the market on faded plaid shirts?

"What kind of flies you tie, Rocky? What's good to use around here?"

"Oh," Rocky said with a wave of his good hand. "I don't know. I just tie some yellow shit on there."

"Rocky," Lew tried after a deep breath. "I'd really like to buy this house. It's an eyesore. Tell you what." He reached in his parka and took out a checkbook. "You take this. It's a blank check. You thought that was only a figure of speech? Well, here it is. You think about our talk and fill in a number, and put this in my mailbox. If it's reasonable, no, scratch that, if it's reasonable times two, you got it. I'll sign it. How's that?"

"No thanks," said Rocky.

Again a deep breath, this time with a sound. "You keep the check. Think on it. Might change your mind." Lew managed a chuckle. "You can always use the money."

"No, sir," said Rocky.

"How's that?"

"I can't use the money. What I need," here with a jerk of his head Rocky indicated the space behind him, "I got."

Lew held steady. "Think about it," he said and left.

That night, Rocky K crossed the road and slipped the check into his neighbor's mailbox, a polished brass affair with an eagle over crossed arrows. Banks charge for checks, he knew that, and he thought Mr. Sheldon might want it back.

Lew Sheldon forewent skiing on that holiday. He spent his time on the phone, arguing with his lawyer, his accountant, both architects, Shawn, and the real estate agent. Somewhere was the right angle.

He left the valley New Year's Day without success. But he was back the first week in March. And again called on Rocky. He put a stack of new hundred dollar bills on the wooden table beside the shotgun loader. He showed Rocky pictures of his house in St. Croix and invited him to use it. He took Rocky down valley and walked him around comparable property he could swap into. He offered to build a replacement house on the very site, at Lew's sole cost.

Nothing.

The right angle came to him by happenstance, with an open face turkey sandwich, cream gravy, mashed potatoes and corn niblets at the Yankee Clipper. He asked his lunch partner, the local broker, how a joint like the diner could survive in so classy a town, and she told him about Doris's lease. Sheldon liked the idea of investing in Cimarron City. He would simply wait her out and have himself a valuable site with commercial zoning when the lease expired. The broker didn't mention the connection between Doris and Rocky K. It wasn't their way to be public about it.

On a Sunday night when Doris and Rocky were sitting at the kitchen table watching a Randolph Scott western on cable, Doris mentioned to Rocky that his neighbor, the one who built the house you could see into? like he was selling cars? was now her landlord.

"That right?" said Rocky. "What does he want with this place, I wonder."

"He doesn't want this. He wants to tear it down, build something new."

Rocky K thought the matter over several days. He recognized pressure when he saw it. The next time he saw Lew Sheldon, pulling out of his glass garage in a Land Rover the colors of the Dust Bin signage, he flagged him down.

"I been thinking," he said. "The new house. I might be interested."

Sheldon could not conceal his delight.

"Well," he said warmly. "We'll do that. A new house, as large as you have now. On the very footpad. We'll give you a separate bathroom and kitchen, and we'll landscape and put gravel in the drive.

And take out . . ." Sheldon's voice trailed off. He meant to say the trash. "What's there," he finished, in an inspiration.

"And this house," Rocky said hesitantly. He had never had to ask anyone for anything in his life. "This house'll be mine?"

"Clear title. No liens or encumbrances. You can do whatever you want with it. Sell it, rent it, tear it down. You're the boss."

There was another issue but Rocky was too proud to raise it. Lew guessed.

"And in the meantime, if you like, you can live at the main house. I'm hardly there. The caretaker unit has a spare room. If you like."

"Well thanks, Mr. Sheldon. Might do that. Depends on when they need me out. The summer, I can bunk with a friend."

"You'll be in by winter. I can promise you that. We'll get right on it."

It was then mid-March, and with Lew's connections he felt safe in his predictions. This job could be slapped up in ninety days, what with no Veronese marble to import, no Philippine mahogany for the banisters. This would be the easiest house he had ever built.

But complications arose. There were the plans. And the regulations—building in the Town of Cimarron City involves hearings, permits, and procedures of Jesuitical complexity. Even for a 1,000 square foot single-family residence, the approvals took time. To top off his troubles, Lew's latest, Shawney the Scrawny he had come to call her, filed for divorce. So it wasn't until mid-September that the construction foreman knocked on the door to Rocky's shack. Finding no one home, he left a note. But Rocky was out fishing—the streams were down in September and the people had gone home—and he never looked for a note when he came back, damp and tired.

Had the Yankee Dollar not closed for the fall, he would have been out at dawn, would have returned to find his house flattened. But as it was, he was scrambling bacon in a pan when he heard the roar of the Cat tractor. He went into the day to find that demolition was beginning.

It took Rocky half an hour to throw everything he owned into the back of the pick-up. Everything except the furniture and the appliances, which they said they'd look after. He rigged a canvas tarp over the truck bed, tied it down, and left his place to the wreckers.

That morning he nailed some timbers out at the Annabelle #6, where it looked like hikers had torn boards off to peek in, maybe even to walk a few feet in the dank air, down the adit to get the feel of a mine. Who the hell would want the feel of a mine? Rocky wondered. Then, since he was in the backcountry and might not get there again before the snows he decided to check two traps and fish Slumgullion Creek. You had to hike four miles down from the site to reach Slumgullion and those same miles uphill to get out, but it'd be worth it.

He stood at the mine portal and looked out. The long spine of the San Cristobals lay before him. It was a magical sight, and he stood a full minute. Off in the distance, way off, a low, dark cloud held as if at anchor. Snow in the high country tonight. He'd already noticed the mosses fading. They turned first, then the high tundra grasses, last the leaves of aspen and cottonwood that brought out the city people and their cameras. It happens every year. Why do they want a picture?

He strung his rod and scrounged about to find some gear packed into the corner of the truck bed. From a tobacco can he picked out three or four pale evening duns. That would be the fly for Slumgullion this time of year. He had tied these a little full, so they would float in the fast water. They were a mayfly imitation, tied with translucent wings of feather the color of hay and a fluffed body from the belly fur of a fox. He'd trimmed that belly strip when he sold the pelt and never got nicked on the price.

Rocky set off down the hill on a game path he had walked before. The afternoon passed as he stood and leapt from rock to rock, watching the wild fish feed and rest, waiting for one to begin its rising cycle. Soon he had two fat brookies and a rainbow strung on a length of willow branch, run through their mouth and gills. That would be dinner for him and the caretaker couple. No sense taking any he couldn't use. Leave them for next time.

When he returned to his truck it was dusk. The storm clouds had rolled closer and were about to swallow the nearest peaks. They blocked most of the sunset, but above and below a few rays shone through like headlights on a highway. There stood the mountains where the crust of the earth had been ripped, where God Himself had torn the rock, crumpled it like a ball of paper and thrown it down at the feet of Rocky Kansas Campaneris.

He would be home after dark.

It was not until he pulled into his drive that he remembered. His house was gone. There, under a sheet of blue plastic he could make out the silhouette of the tub and toilet. But where the house had stood there was only a concrete slab, swept clean as a trailer pad. He backed out the pickup and pulled into Lew Sheldon's drive.

Something was different here, too. The house was dark. He reached the front door and found a paper taped by the oversized brass horseshoe that was the knocker. This will be for me, he thought. It'll tell me how I get in. He pulled the paper off, lit a match, and held it close.

It wasn't for him. It was something called a Writ of Distraint, and it had something to do with a lawsuit filed in New York County Supreme Court, Trial Term. He saw Shawn's name and Mr. Sheldon's. He pasted it back on the door as best he could. The wind was cold, and it was beginning to snow, the first of the year, so the tape didn't take.

Damn, he thought. Doris is gone for the season and I got no place else to go. There were motels in town, Bed and Breakfasts they were now called, but they charged five times what a bed ought to cost and Rocky didn't carry that much cash. And of course he didn't own a credit card.

He got back in the cab of his truck, took off his shoes and put them under his head for a pillow, and curled up on the seat. The heater had broken at the end of last winter and he had not yet looked to it, and the window wouldn't close all the way on the shotgun side, ever since that drunk in Casper kicked in the door. Still, he'd slept in the truck before and God knows he'd slept in worse.

He dreamed he was skiing. He hadn't skied since he was a kid, but he dreamed he was skiing with Doris. They'd do it the way he used to: one pair of skis, wide, wooden ones with a bear claw binding you'd strap on and wind around the ankle in a figure eight so they wouldn't come off. In the dream she drove him up the hill in the pickup and he hopped out and skied down while she drove down the road to get him. Then it would be her turn and he would drive the truck. Just like when he was a kid. Except his legs were the same length. No more limp. The leg hurt where it grew, but then it stopped hurting. He made long serpentines in the snow, the powder seeping into his boots, and he gathered speed and jumped off the frame of the mine portal, the way they used to. He was flying.

He woke up to the sound of breaking glass. Outside was white. Fourteen inches had fallen during the night, and his feet were covered with snow come in through the gap in the window. His feet had fallen deep asleep, the only sensation a dull ache.

Across the way, the construction crew was loading what was left of his shack into a dumpster. He sat up stiffly, brushed the snow off his socks, and tried to get his boots on. Frozen, feet and boots alike, and he knew if he forced either one his toes would crumble like cold toast. He sat there in the white chrysalis of his truck. The front windshield was covered and the window on his side sparkled frost to its top. He sat there and was warmed by his anger. It would be the second time since he'd met this fellow Sheldon that he would have to ask somebody's help.

He reached in his pocket and fished out a cigarette, lit it and inhaled. Then he leaned over and rolled down the far window.

"Mornin'," he yelled. The workers stopped loading and looked over at him. "One of you guys spare a minute? I think my feet are froze."

• • •

For a long time, only a few people outside the hospital knew he was confined there. People at Summit, who had to verify the insurance information. They notified the union steward, but the steward was a new man, new maybe six years ago, and didn't know this reclusive fellow who manned an outpost with no mining. So he paid no mind. Rocky knew where Doris was, visiting her sister in Tucumcari, but the address was in the truck, tucked in the crate with the canned peaches. Besides, he felt a damn fool and there was nothing she could do. Not as if she had an extra foot.

He lay in the hospital down valley, in a room with five other men. They came and went, one he was sure died, but no one let on. The doctors came and went, too, inspecting the God-awful blisters on his feet, waiting to see what would happen. Trouble with frostbite was, once you were exposed you were more susceptible. That would work a bucketful of hell on a man whose only job left in life was walking into mining claims in the Colorado mountains.

Finally they made their decision. They were looking for gangrene and the right foot came back clean, pink and hurting as though someone with a rail spike got curious about it. But the left didn't and they had to take a couple of toes. They said he was lucky to save the rest and he guessed as how he was.

"Shee-it," he said to the doctor and held up his short hand. "With my shoes off, I can still count to fifteen."

County Hospital kept him a long time. To make sure that the good foot had taken and that the circulation wouldn't collapse. And then there was physical therapy: losing toes does funny things to your balance. Since they had come off what was a short leg to begin with, the doctor told him he would have trouble at first. He did, and nightly he felt a phantom pain in the toes that were gone.

A week before his discharge he had his first visitor. Doris had come back. The season was starting, and he figured she had come early to stock and staff the Clipper for the winter months. It would be good to have her back, apple pie for breakfast and Sunday nights in front of her television.

But he was wrong. Doris had returned only to wind up. She had sold the rest of her lease to Mr. Sheldon and she was hanging up the apron.

"I've had enough of it, Rocky K," she told him. "Work your ass off and at the end of the year you've got just enough to open next year and do it again. What's the sense of it?"

She was moving to Tucumcari, where her sister lived. With the money from Mr. Sheldon, she was buying a franchise to do tax returns. "No gravy, no yesterday's vegetables for tomorrow's soup. Just paper, can you imagine? Ain't that a dream?"

Rocky K was sure that Sheldon had forced her out, but had he asked she would have told him no. Mr. Sheldon couldn't have been nicer. Mr. Sheldon was sorry to see her go. Still, he would be razing the property for a new building and had already found a tenant to take her place. Two young men already in the restaurant business in Carmel, California. Doris showed Rocky their ad in the newspaper. Contemporary cuisine in casual elegance.

• • •

Rocky K was released in the first week of December. He found his truck in the hospital lot. Doris had retrieved it. The three fish he'd given to the fellow who had driven him to the hospital. Everything else was there under the lashed tarp. He didn't have to check. He recognized his knots.

He set out to Buffalo Mountain. The clutch felt foreign and slippery under his altered foot. He drove through Cimarron City, its streets crowded with families of skiers dressed in bright colors and fake furs. Everyone was carrying paper bags bearing the names of stores. Where do you suppose they put all that shit? Rocky wondered. He drove past the site of the Yankee Dollar. Opening Soon, said the sign in the new window. The Green Snail.

He wound up the hill towards his home site and pulled in the drive. It was gravel, just as Mr. Sheldon had promised. And the house. Completed. Rocky K looked at it, stunned.

It was a replica of Sheldon's house. A perfect replica, accomplished to a fraction of scale. One story, divided with steel beams to look like four. Even the cantilevered wings, Rocky's so small they couldn't be used, merely glass appendages. The front door was open. Workmen were laying carpet in its main room. Rocky stood and called from the doorway.

"Excuse me."

A bearded workman wearing kneepads over his jeans got off the floor and came to the door.

"Help you?"

"Who're you?"

"Cimarron City Carpets. Who're you?"

"Campaneris. My place."

"How 'bout that? Everyone's wondering where you been. You been away for off season?"

"Yeah. I been away."

"Caretaker said you may show up. Figured you were out in the backcountry. Seeing to your mines. Look, Mr. Campaneris, we're just finishing up. Gas and electric's hooked up. You can move right in. We'll be out by noon."

"Where's the caretaker?"

"He and his wife drove down to Denver to grocery shop. Sheldon is coming up next week with his new wife. That model divorced him. You probably didn't hear, you been gone. Divorced him, even locked up his house for a week."

"I heard," Rocky K said. "No one in their house?"

"You mean the main house? No. Be back tomorrow. You want to come in and look around? You got some view."

Through the bare room Rocky K looked out. He could see the far window and beyond the San Cristobal range, covered in fresh snow. It was the same view he had before.

"Yep," he said. "See you."

Rocky K sat in his truck and thought. Not about what he was going to do. He thought about skiing over those old mineshafts and how you had to wind the Arlberg straps so they were just right. He thought about what he would do if he had a chicken to fry just then, how Doris would make it for him with sliced turnip and a quartered onion, and how they would drink whiskey while the whole mess fried on the stove. It made him hungry, and angry too, for he had no place to do just that.

He let down the tailgate of the truck and found the box of canned goods. He took out four jars of red cabbage and dumped the cabbage on the new snow. Then he fired up the truck—had to lift the hood and open up the choke to get her to turn over—and set out to the Cornstalk #2. He drove as far as the plowed county road would take him, got out and knocked in the axles to engage the front wheels, and took off up the dirt road to the claim. He searched through the keys on his ring and found the one for the padlock. Inside the shed, shelved neatly where he had stowed them, were exactly what he needed. He took out the scale, set it level on a board in the snow. Then he measured out 320 grams of ammonium nitrate four times and poured it equally into the four empty cabbage jars. He broke the seal on a plastic jug and measured 128 grams of nitromethane liquid for each jar. It had been a while but he was confident. He moved the jars softly so the liquid flowed and soaked into the powder equally, forming a pink dough. Then he screwed on the lids and put the jars on the seat of the cab beside him. He walked back to the shed, took half a dozen number six caps from the steel box, and locked everything up. Four pounds worth. Ought to be about right.

He drove back as darkness settled over the town. Up on Buffalo Mountain you could see into town as the lights of the restaurants and discos came on, the bars with their flickering signs and pounding music. There was still enough light to work. He went up to the Sheldons' house just to be sure. There were no cars in the drive and no one answered the knock of the urn-sized horseshoe.

Then he walked back to his house. It was his, Mr. Sheldon had said so. He placed a jar by each corner, with a cap in its open mouth, and made his connections. He lifted the truck hood a second time, ran the wires off its battery to the far side, and lay down in the snow. Nestled with the truck between him and the new house, hot wires in one hand, firing wires in the other.

The four blasts were almost simultaneous, a hair of a second off. A cosmic drum roll cracked across the space. It sucked the breath from his chest and drove the ambient air right out of the sky leaving nothing to breathe. Like falling into a cold stream. It was, he remembered from the smell and the sound and the adrenaline, why powder men loved their work.

Below in the town, some people heard a single blast, others swore six. The theories on what caused it also went wide of the mark, from a sonic boom to an airline crash. Most popular guess was that someone had torched the gasoline storage tanks up on Buffalo Mountain, the ones built during the oil crisis by a famous entertainer and environmentalist.

Rocky K had overestimated. Several of his neighbors on the hill lost a few windows. Fortunately, zoning on Buffalo Mountain requires that houses protect themselves from each other with distance and berms. Except for the Sheldon house, and of course Rocky's, which disappeared, damage was slight.

But Lew Sheldon's house was directly in the path of the concussion. The explosions knocked out virtually every pane. Glass fell in five bedrooms and six baths, in the caretaker's quarters, the media room, the pub, the library, and in the master suite on the topmost floor. Shards of glass fell in the living room on the steel and brass coffee table with the black horn top and cracks appeared in the glass doors of the embossed lizard-leather etagere. Splinters fell softly into the crevices of the sofas, covered in Boussac print, into the conversation pit, and with a plink into the Chinese crackle-glaze bowl. They fell around the small iron sculpture by Louise Nevelson, making it look quite pretty, like a small Christmas tree, and bounced harmlessly off the Second Century Hellenistic torso and onto the Louis XVI-style bureau plat below. Slivers fell without noise on the Aubusson carpets in the living room and on the French needlepoint rugs in the dining room. They tinkled and fell into the two-person marble tub and into the Sherle Wagner onyx sink fashioned like a scallop shell. And they fell on the Clarence House silk bed cover in the master suite that had not yet been rolled down and on the top of the canopy of the magnificent Chippendale period carved four-poster, where they were not found for months.

The explosion blew glass into the house and into the garage too, where splinters tinkled off the Land Rover, festive with its Dust Bin insignia, and off the black Saab sedan and the maroon Jaguar convertible, polished to a military shine. And tiny nettles of glass fell into the indoor pool and settled on its floor. The vacuum would suck up most of them, but eventually, to get them all, the pools had to be emptied and swept, and that is when traces of glass were found outside. For the two pools were connected, so that swimmers could wander from one to the other, emerging into the fresh mountain air under a waterfall created by moss rock and a pump. And slivers of glass had been carried outdoors by the faint current.

SETTING IT TIGHT

ON DRY LAND

Everyone in town seemed to fly fish, so the idea of the ad lured him. A free lesson on casting, provided by the local fly shop. One hour, novice to expert, rod and reel supplied. Several guides would be on hand, to provide individual instruction.

He protected his Saturday routine—a run, errands like the Laundromat and the bank, lunch alone, and an afternoon to indulge in novels, usually Trollope or Dickens. But this week May arrived and it promised to burst with hope and blossom and new growth. So Bernard stretched through his sun salutes, jogged his jog, showered, breakfasted his breakfast, and located the park on his city map. Donned his sun hat and his sunglasses, and patted 30 plus protective lotion on the back of his neck—he tended to burn. Should he shave? No need. It was a Saturday, followed by a Saturday night, followed by a Sunday, and he had no other plans. The laundry and the groceries could as well be done by a new him, a him that was an incipient fly fisherman. Fly fishermen, in his mind's eye, did not bother to shave on Saturdays.

He noticed it first on his run, over the usual route. It seemed that, with the sunshine and lurid warmth, all the other joggers had paired off. He had no explanation. It was not as if there was anything to say when you're jogging. And if there was, he had heard it—tight calves, shin splints, where you carry your keys.

Still, he noticed. And again in the park: couples on bicycles, on foot, on in-line skates. Even the cabbage moths seemed to be auditioning for the Disney Channel.

He was minutes late. Equally divided between men and women, the group had circled around the owner of the fly shop. Bernard approached and peered in. The man was describing the morning's agenda. Fly fishing, he pronounced, was the art of pursuit. It consisted of enticing the unsuspecting prey into self-deceit.

"The fish respects a good presentation. Nature respects artifice."

He would talk more about philosophy later. Twice as many as expected had shown up, he explained, so one half of them could wait. Or better, they could pair off and share instructors and equipment.

"You'll get plenty of casting time," he assured them. "If you want more practice, come down to the shop and throw a line in our parking lot."

Bernard had dabbled in self-help courses and had never cared for them: self-help in his case was usually inadequate. Still, plunge on. He did as he was told, and lined up self-consciously behind two pretty girls. They chattered to each other and avoided eye contact. He considered whether he shouldn't switch to a fragrance-free sun cream. Behind him, a tall fellow in a pink collared tee shirt began talking.

"I want to try that new compound they're using," he announced. "I'm all for new concepts." Bernard turned to find his nose inches from a tiny embroidered polo player.

"Take the boron rods," the man said. "They were a bust. I bought one and used it twice. It sits in the hall closet." Bernard's hope that the man was talking to someone else died with the next sentence, clearly a confidence directed at him.

"Set me back six hundred bucks."

Bernard turned back quickly and kept his eyes forward.

They neared the front of the queue where the owner was dispensing rods and reels. A single man stood aside, looking to partner.

"Are you together?" the owner asked.

"Oh, yes," one of the girls said. "Don't separate us." Bernard caught the man's eye, to volunteer himself, but the gesture was lost. A boy from the line was called up to complete the pair, and Bernard found himself wed for the morning to the man with the rod in the closet. As if to cement the union, the man leaned forward and, to Bernard's mystification, said in a low voice, "It's a nine for a nine."

A single rod was issued to the pretty girls who disappeared giggling, and a second, reel attached, to Bernard and his partner.

"Here you go fellas," the man said. "Enjoy."

"Since we're going to spend the day together, my name's Cliff." The boron man took the rod from Bernard's hand and flexed it knowingly. "Not bad. But not what I came for."

They strolled to the card table where the shop was capturing names for its mailing list. There they were to rendezvous with their instructor.

"Why don't you go back and ask?" Bernard suggested helpfully. "I'm sure if you ask they'll give you what you want."

Cliff looked past him. "Why don't I?" he asked, a narrow-eyed glint sharpening his face. He had the toothy good looks of a TV sportscaster, and a tan weeks ahead of the season. He pointed with his chin. "That's why."

"What is it you want?"

Bernard turned again to find their instructor at his elbow. She was an angel in quick-dry khaki. Her bright eyes moved from Cliff to him and quickly back. She wore knee-length shorts and a shirt with the logo of the fly shop on one pocket. Above the other "Kristin" was stitched in red. Worn by another, her outfit—climbing boots and rag socks—might suggest androgyny. Kristin was unmistakably feminine.

"Oh," said Cliff, giving the words a heavy read, "I'll be sure to let you know. When we know each other better."

Kristin allowed a seedling smile, spun and signaled them to follow. How is it, Bernard wondered, that women who should know better swing at the dumbest pitches?

She led them to a large meadow where the group had spread out. Instructors were earnestly at work with their pupils. Calligraphic arcs of tangerine and white and turquoise bloomed in the air against dark leafing elms. Behind the row of casters, close to the trees, a couple lay necking on a blanket. Nearby a second couple lazily tossed a Frisbee.

Kristin asked something. He was studying a lock of hair that threatened to fall across her extraordinary brow, and he missed the question.

"Bernard," he guessed.

"I'm sorry," she said and flashed the tip of a tongue. "I asked what level you were."

"Level." Did she mean his apartment? He didn't want to risk another show of inattention.

"Casting. What level?"

"I've done a lot of fishing," Cliff interrupted. "South Andros, Christmas Island, Los Roques." He gave the "r" in Roques an ample roll. "But I'm sure there are things you can teach me."

"And you? It's Bernard?"

"Yes. Bernard. Well, it said novices too. So," and here he shrugged, wishing he hadn't. "I'm a novice. I thought maybe I could learn . . ."

"Of course. That's the point, isn't it."

She suggested she start with Cliff, who was already laying out line. He was saying words that meant nothing to Bernard, steeple casts, punches, double hauling, or was it double-alling? Cliff's casts seemed to go wherever he willed them. He placed line down on the grass in a perfect S and handed the rod to her to try. Bernard feared they might be working their way through the alphabet. Soon the two were laughing, as first Cliff then she tried to behead dandelions thirty yards away.

No, no, he told her. Just lower the rod. Like this.

Cliff had his arms about her, his hands holding hers on the cork grip. Cuddled spoon in spoon, they might have been new-found love in a 'Forties musical. Bernard began to contemplate his laundry.

At last Cliff looped a clump of dandelions, tightened, and cut them down.

"Bernard, your turn." She was flushed from pleasure. He approached cautiously, diffidently. Could he decline, say he'd changed his mind? What was the point on a lovely May morning when there were only weeds to catch? Besides, he never really cared for fish.

"Not so tight, don't strangle it, and put the thumb like this," he heard her saying. "Now, just relax, and get some line out."

Bernard waved the rod the way he thought Cliff had. Coils grew at his feet and the line draped impotently to the ground, refusing to take to the air. Had they changed something on him, flicked a switch? This rig didn't seem to work.

"No, no. Don't work so hard. It's in the wrist, not the hips. Listen to the rod, feel the timing."

Bernard had no idea what she meant. There was no timing to feel. And the rod wasn't saying anything to him.

"It's not working, Kristin." Cliff's voice was unctuous with understanding. "Let's start him out with a roll cast." Bernard's cheeks, already moist from the effort, reddened and warmed. A roll cast sounded subservient to a full cast. He didn't change his mind when Kristin demonstrated one by flipping a hoop of line that rolled like a surfer's curl and laid forty feet straight ahead. Still, the abbreviated motion seemed a trick for the disadvantaged, something you'd see on Jerry Lewis's Telethon.

When Bernard tried it, the loop inexplicably got tangled in the elastic cord that held his sunglasses.

"Not everyone can get this," Cliff said, his sympathy deep as Saran Wrap. "Different strokes. That's why some people dangle worms from piers. There's no shame in that."

"Let's regroup," Kristin said. She was trying for optimism, but Bernard heard in her voice the wooden throb of futility. "Let's put a marker on the end of the line so you can see where it's supposed to go."

She reeled in quickly and took from her pocket an inch square of stiff red cloth. Tied it on in seemingly a single motion and bit off the short end.

"Now that will be your fly. You watch that red square and don't go into the forward cast until it approaches the end of the back cast. The whole object," and she put five yards of line in the air, "is to keep the line in motion by loading the rod." She spoke in kindergarten rhythms on each stroke. "Keep . . .the rod . . .loaded . . .and it . . .does all . . .the work."

Bernard stood feeling the dunce as her line floated by. A hot spot ticked on the heel of his hand, warning of a blister. He glanced at her watch. The advertisement had said ten to eleven. Could he make it through the hour without strangling himself? Maybe Cliff could be convinced to take a second try at open-air seduction.

"Now," she said in the voice of a missionary offering salvation, "that's all there is to it."

She held the rod out to him. He removed his sun hat, took off his glasses, folded them inside the hat and placed both on the grass. He looked at his palm—sure enough, on its heel was an angry red blotch the size of a quarter. Still, he took the rod and again started trying to whip the imaginary lion.

"There," she called when the close half of line went by in the beginning of a bulge. But by the time he sparked at her encouragement, slack had gathered and now flagged back and forth at his feet. She came and put her hand above his on the rod.

"Not so much work, Bernard. Easy, take your time, enjoy yourself. Just relax. It's like making love."

With that he gave a Herculean jerk. Energized, the red square came flying back and popped him in the eye.

"Ow," he cried and dropped the rod.

"That one got away," said Cliff with a snort.

The eye throbbed and teared. He wished he were anywhere but here. At the laundry, even on a river. Don't all rivers run to the sea?

Kristin inspected the eye. She insisted on wetting down a sterile square of gauze, making a cold compress, insisted on taping the eye shut.

Later that afternoon she phoned to make sure he was all right. Of course he was, but she could not have been more concerned. She even offered to teach him individually if he would come around the fly shop.

"I'm sure we could get you there," she said. "You were just on the verge."

Bernard did not come to the fly shop for a lesson. He did drop in, more than once. But he never picked up a fly rod again.

• • •

Later, when they took fishing trips, and they did, often as a family, he took Dickens or Trollope and read on a blanket by the stream.

And when they related the story to friends who asked, to their children who wanted to hear it again, Bernard told it eye-poke and all. They found the outcome charming, serendipitous, but he dismissed them, saying Kristin had it in mind from the start.

"All part of the pursuer and the prey. I ask you, have you ever heard such a come-hither line? Here's this beautiful girl telling me, Relax, it's like making love. Can you imagine? It's a wonder I didn't put out both my eyes."

RISING UNDER THE BRIDGE

THE GREEN
LANTERN

Cobwebs of family, business, and sport connected the eight men who gathered at Glen Gillen Lodge. At the center of the web, Gib Alexander knew all but one. Indeed it was he who had assembled the group. Had schooled with some, sailed with others, and fished with each. All but the one. Gib did not flinch at taking the occasional stage as God's understudy, it was natural for him, he enjoyed taking command. And he trusted his own judgment, knew they would make a companionable and interesting table.

At the very least, they all shared one trait: wealth. Most would consider a week at Glen Gillen an extravagance. It boasted a Cordon Bleu kitchen, a cellar that would be the envy of most of the Michelin shortlist, ghillies who would, if asked, carry you down the bank and back, and eight glorious beats on one of Scotland's famous salmon rivers.

Arranging lives was simply one of Gibson Alexander's talents—economic advisor to two presidents, contributor to magazines of learned opinion, and, for ten years now, dean of the business school at an Eastern university of some repute. He had constructed this group the way he might have selected an incoming class: politics a gap sufficiently diffuse for tolerant debate but no wider; a passion for the endeavor, in this case Atlantic salmon rather than the study of profit; and a capacity to contribute to the comradeship. All, of course, but the one.

There had been a last-minute cancellation. An old boardroom mate of Gib's had suffered a recurrence of angina, and Alexander, intrigued by the introduction of randomness into his stacked deck, sent out an e-mail to the participants asking for a quick substitute. First come, first served, he announced.

The first to come forth was his cousin, Hiram Beedle.

"I've been spending a lot of time with a client." A corporate lawyer, Hiram had an unpleasantly practical streak. "His company just joined the Exchange. We were on the floor yesterday. He got to ring the bell."

What, Gib wondered, had all this to do with the man's credentials as a fishing partner?

"Anyway, he said as how he would love to try it."

"Try it?" Gib did not keep the skepticism out of his voice.

"Oh he's used a fly rod before. Has a place in the Adirondacks. Stocks panfish. Said he'd love to try salmon."

Quite a different kettle, thought Gib. But he had announced the opening, and it needed filling. Otherwise he would have to stand the considerable difference with the booking agency.

"Very well," Gib told Beedle and picked up a pen to note the particulars.

Joseph Torino, he wrote. A town and a country address. Several phones, cells, fax numbers.

"Torino. Do I know his name?"

"Torino Cheeses."

"I beg your pardon?"

"Torino Cheeses. That's what he gave out on the floor of the Exchange. A basket of their Parmesan. The company services most of the restaurants in New York and New Jersey. Not just cheeses. Bakery stuff, canned meats, he's even getting into laundry supplies and full kitchen packages."

"Is he?"

"But he made his start with cheeses. They are, you might say, his foundation."

Gib knew Beedle to be a humorless man, so he swallowed his words. He had invited Beedle after a not inconsiderable deliberation, for the man was earnest to a fault, taciturn, and narrow of interest. But he was a sportsman—Alexander had fished with him in Norway and New Brunswick. Every table needed listeners as well as talkers.

And most of the others were talkers. The Robards brothers, Tennessee gentlemen, favored political argument and in that endeavor ably represented the Eighteenth Century. The world they admired had been diminished by hydroelectric dams, the creation in 1913 of the federal income tax, and dilution of the United States Constitution by some twenty-seven amendments.

For every trip that Gib planned, Richard Rassenall received an invitation. An architect by training, Rassenall was a storyteller by disposition. He stood six-six in stocking waders, could cast a line halfway across the Atlantic, and claimed an interest in clarets, shotguns, and epic poetry that some reserved for grandchildren.

Regulars from past trips filled the last two slots. Dorough, whose habit of calling everyone by surname, in the English style, had erased in Gib's memory Dorough's Christian name; and Leland Kells.

Dorough was good company. Limited though good. His conversation rarely reached anything beyond fly fishing, but on hatches, casts, conditions, strategies, knots, fly selection, line weights, entomology, equipment, and such ichthyologic nuances as the ocular structure of tarpon versus trout, he was eloquent.

Gib had reservations about Leland Kells. Despite, or perhaps because of, his fortune—the name Kells was stamped on the brass strike plates of most American doors—Kells managed to make every outing a competition. Still, he was a distant relative of the Robards brothers, a client of Beedle's, and his presence on a dozen of these trips established his credentials for this group.

• • •

Life at Glen Gillen followed a set ritual. Breakfast at seven, on the river by nine. Lunch streamside with one's ghillie, occasionally joined by the guide and fisherman from a neighboring beat. Off the river by seven for a long cocktail hour and a nine o'clock dinner served family style. Bed, and rise at six to do it again. At dinner they were served by the cook, Mrs. Phillips, and joined by the head ghillie. Keith MacPherson would open the river log, and with the diligence of a cicerone record the day's catch, the dimensions of the fish, and the successful lure.

There inevitably followed a discussion of what fly the fish were favoring and which they ignored. The debate given to choice of fly put the doctrine in a place of centrality akin to that of transubstantiation in the Mother Church.

So it was, after the first day, abnormally bright for autumn in the highlands, the hillsides lit to a lavender radiance and the river running copper and clear, that everyone quizzed Hiram Beedle on his, the only catch registered.

"It was a fifteen-pound hen. She brushed the fly twice. I had to go back, shorten up, go back again."

"And she took?"

"A Green Lantern."

Hiram repeated the story three more times as anglers wandered into the lounge, and a fourth for Keith MacPherson at table.

Joe Torino joined the dinner mid-conversation. He had not shaved that morning, and by now sported the blue-black chin of a torpedo in a mob movie. One of the Robards brothers suggested he remove his baseball cap.

"Torino Cheese," he said and jerked his thumb towards its insignia, a wheel of cheddar behind a scrolled TC. "You wear the hat, you deduct the trip. Business expense."

"A Green Lantern," mused the other Robards. "That's a dark horse. Tie one up for me, will you Keith?"

Several others asked for a Lantern.

"Aye," Keith agreed. "I'll tie them after dinner."

"You can't really believe," Torino addressed the table, "the salmon cares what crap is on the end of the line. These are fish, remember? They shit where they breathe."

Silence fell across the planed boards. The men looked down at their hands or to their drinks. As senior member, Gib Alexander sent Hiram the slightest nod. Torino was, after all, Beedle's guest, and as in any club a host stood responsible for the behaviour of his guest.

"The choice of fly," said Hiram softly, "is an important aspect of salmon fishing."

"How do you know?"

"I beg your pardon?" Beedle believed his statement sufficient on its face, and was surprised when Torino failed to accept it without question.

"How do you know? At the lake I catch bluegills on a bare hook. This is some asshole fish. It hasn't evolved since Jesus was a corporal. A brain the size of a pea."

Hiram Beedle took a breath. Equanimity was a hallmark of his law practice. In the most fractious negotiations he remained infrangibly civil. The tactic was more than a matter of breeding—it served a purpose, for in these transactions, often involving strong feelings and considerable sums, both sides often came to regard his judgment as neutral.

"The sport has a history," Beedle began. "It goes back, we don't know how far, the pursuit of wild fish with an artificial lure. The Egyptians. It's mentioned in Plutarch. Why, Isaac Walton, in Sixteen . . ." and Beedle looked about.

"Sixteen fifty-three," Alexander put in.

"Sixteen fifty-three, takes pains about the choice of fly. Not merely pattern, but size, color . . ."

"Yeah, yeah. I've heard." Torino twisted the peak of his cap about to lean closer to his soup. "Count me in, Keith. Tie one up for me."

"Not a difficult tie," said the ghillie. "If the Lantern turns out to be the magic fly, we are prepared. I have three spools of green tinsel." The men who had ordered the fly rested easier.

"And take heart, gentlemen. Tomorrow will bring a change in the sky. We'll nae have so many skunks returning to the lodge."

"You guaranty that?" Rassanall boomed good-naturedly.

"Aye, sir. With the chill, Lord Salmon will begin to move."

• • •

The head ghillie proved right. The next day clouds thick as plaster lowered into the valley and sat, immobile as the hills. The same water that had gleamed copper from peat when the sun was on it paled silver and opaque. As if to celebrate the turn of cold, salmon breeched freely, and the sight of their celebration quickened every fisherman's breath.

That evening, bottles of Lagavulin and Balvenie and the Macallan passing about, the men found that six fish had been netted by three fisherman. One of the Robards had caught a twelve-pound cock in the morning. Leland Kells had caught both a grilse and a full-grown fish. Torino, the novice, had caught three.

And all six had taken a Green Lantern.

At dinner, Keith MacPherson took tying requests from everyone. Whatever the reason, these fish had decided that the oddly dressed Lantern, its Kelly green sides imitating nothing in nature, was the prey they wanted to devour.

"I'll put out a few dozen," Keith said. "Tying in bulk goes faster."

The dinner-table mood was joyous. Fish were moving, the weather had settled like concrete, and there were five days of fishing left.

Richard Rassenall stood and recited "The Shooting of Dangerous Dan McGrew," and Mrs. Phillips was persuaded to sing "My Heart's in the Highlands." Her thin and sweet soprano made the men, in a moment, Scottish and homesick.

Moved by his day's success and an amplitude of single-malt, Joe Torino decided to join in the entertainment. He rose and sang "The Winnipeg Whore." Its increasingly vivid lyric sent Gib Alexander to the kitchen to engage Mrs. Phillips in a discussion of the proper way to butterfly a leg of lamb, lest she overhear the happy grocer's words. But on the whole, the evening was a pleasant one, the most pleasant, as it turned out, the group would spend.

• • •

For breakfast Wednesday produced a startling announcement.

"The spools of tinsel," said Keith, "are not there." The ghillie clenched his teeth and let the news settle. "Perhaps I misplaced them. Or perhaps one of you borrowed them," his voice took on the timbre of a Methodist minister, "and these words will serve to remind you of their return."

Keith had tied surrogates, winding the same pattern as the Lantern but with yellow tinsel on some and blue on others. He distributed them to a visibly alarmed group.

"Maybe these will do," Dorough said to the Robardses as they left the dining room. "In the water the blue could look green."

"And I could look like Tom Cruise," said one of the brothers, "but I don't."

"Well," Dorough looked for consolation. "Whoever borrowed the tinsel from Keith's bench will return it."

"Don't be naive. If you were merely tying your own, you'd do it at the bench. Or you'd take one spool. You wouldn't need three."

The weather held. A pewter sky over a pewter river, leaping fish and no wind. When the eight men assembled for whisky before dinner the stories of plenty and famine produced darker reactions. Four fisherman had caught fish—Kells and a Robards one each, Torino and Gib Alexander two. And the authentic Green Lantern was responsible for all six fish. The yellow and blue substitutes had been flown and swum, flown and drifted, flown and jigged, all to no avail.

Like air to a fire, whisky will make a pleasant disposition flame to joy, but it can smolder a dark mood. Mindful of his headmaster's annual sermon on obligation, Gib Alexander insisted that Dorough take his Green Lantern the following day. The Robards brothers agreed to fish together and share. If these were lifeboat survivors and the flies the last sips in the canteen, the remaining store of Green Lanterns could not have been more in their thoughts.

That night moisture off the Gulf Stream flowed into a sag of Arctic air. Over the dark soil of Scotland, heavy-bellied clouds smelling of damp piled into the Highland glens. By the time the men approached the river, bearing their Spey rods like spear-carriers, a sharp and icy rain was slanting down. Each man and guide turned high his collar, tied his hood beneath his chin, donned his fingerless gloves. And forded in to do battle.

But the fraternity of the shared flies soon turned sour. On his second cast Robards the borrower, doubtless excited by his chance at success, put too much muscle into the back cast. There was a crack like the bullet of an assassin. Hapless, he turned to the bank where his brother and two ghillies looked on in shock. No need to explain—he had snapped off the Lantern. Robards the lender spread a tarpaulin on the ground, and the three men sat down wordlessly to pass another fishless day.

Richard Rassenall had at least some success. His borrowed Lantern caught him two good fish—mid teens in weight and fresh from the sea—before Rassenall, in a lapse of reverie to which fishermen are prone, allowed his retrieve to wander. The fly snagged on a sunken log and Rassenall broke it off. He and his ghillie spent a precious hour shuffling through the stream to find the branch, without success.

• • •

The mood of Thursday's cocktail hour resembled that of the command tent of an army in retreat. Reports from Kells and Torino, fishing the survivor Lanterns, of three salmon each, no longer brought cries of congratulation, and instead added to the disconsolation. The Lanternless gathered in small glowering knots muttering their speculation. Sinister glances found their way to Joe Torino.

"I say search his room," said Dorough. "Why spend a fishless week standing on ceremony? No bill of rights here."

"Now, now," counseled Beedle. "We have no evidence. Besides, Keith has called London. They're expressing two dozen Lanterns and three spools up tomorrow."

"Saturday," corrected the skunked Robards. "No flights into Aberdeen until Saturday."

"And Sunday's a half-day," noted Dorough with uncharacteristic intensity.

Alexander overheard the seditious talk and stepped in. Gib was a man of highly developed manners. He had hunted with princes. He played the cello well, kept a tame monkey, and had designed and planted an English garden. And was considered by all who knew him a connoisseur in human felicity.

Yet he found himself unable to dissuade the budding vigilantes.

"We cannot be peremptory," he cautioned. "Remember that both he and Kells had a Green Lantern to start."

"That's just it," Dorough said. "He's an amateur. No amateur could do this on one fly. He must have lost several. Yet he's still fishing a Lantern."

Gib's efforts at rapprochement were not aided at dinner. Keith announced the following day's beats and ghillies, as usual, and added a nettlesome footnote. "At the rate he's going, Mr. Torino might set the record for one week's catch."

"This year's record?"

"No, Mister Beedle. For so long as we've been keeping track. It goes back to Culludden and the banning of the kilts."

Torino must have sensed the tide of resentment, for he lowered his eyes to his plate. Only Kells commented, and that with a warning.

"I'm right behind him."

"That's as it is, sir. Only two fish behind with two and a half days to go."

"And if either one of us loses his fly . . ." Kells said hopefully. Everyone knew how the unfinished sentence would end: there would be no replacements until Saturday night.

Dorough leaned over the table and whispered. The Robards brothers patted Kells' arm in encouragement.

Alexander watched them carefully. If anyone were up to mischief it would be they. Beedle put too high a stake on the law to do anything rash. Kells was catching fish, and Rassenall, he hoped, would consider searching another man's luggage unseemly.

Though he could sense they all had some sympathy with the idea. As, Alexander had to admit, he himself was beginning to feel.

The distance between the men and Torino grew in the lounge after dinner. Fishing talk inflamed passion under the circumstances, and talk of politics had been exhausted. In one clutch, glasses rosy with the Macallan, the talk turned—as it does in such circles—to college life.

"I myself," said Kells of a particular club at a particular school, "was in . . ." and he mentioned a college society. The words sounded quaint and distant.

Rassenall was clearly pleased. "Excellent," he smiled broadly. "As was I." At the discovery, they moved inches closer, and soon afterwards inches more, when they found that they had also shared failed hopes for a more prominent club.

"I must tell you," Rassenall confided to him about the group that had spurned them, "they took a particularly rum lot my year."

Kells quickly agreed. His eyes shone with disappointment, fresh as it was when he was twenty, and he looked eagerly to the taller man for any derogatory news. "My year too. Rum is the word." He leaned over his glass as if he might spit in his drink. "Still, I should have been asked. I deserved to be. My grandfather was a member."

"What's the topic?" asked Joe Torino.

"Clubs," Rassenall told him. "Silly stuff, really. We find we went to the same university and belonged to the same club."

"Ah," said Joe Torino. "I've joined Kiwanis."

• • •

At Friday breakfast the table enjoyed none of the bonhomie of the earlier days. Yet the weather—drizzly, dismal and frosting cold—was perfect for Atlantic salmon. Even the technical chatter had a mordant and hopeless tone to it.

Joe Torino sat at the end of the table. Neither seat by him was occupied. He listened to the Robards brothers discuss the paltry choice of flies left to them.

"Why don't you take my fly?" he broke in. "I've got lots of them."

"Lots? You have more Green Lanterns?" They couldn't believe their ears, and turned to him with the enthusiasm of Javier. The burglar was giving himself in.

"No. I have just the one. I meant fish. I've caught lots of them."

Kells stood behind their end of the table, ladling eggs and sweet sausage from a chafing dish. "But there's the record," he said.

"Aaah," Torino waved his hand as if to chase a mosquito. "Listen. I'd freeze my ass off for record profits. Or for the record of screws in a single night." He took a mouthful of porridge and spoke through it.

"But fish?"

The brothers did not respond to his offer. Torino made it to others and was met with the same demurral, the same muffled hostility. He decided the rebuff must be recognition of his earlier point, that salmon can't possibly care what fly one uses.

That afternoon cocktails began early. A week of successful fishing in Scotland is a mother lode of anecdotes, a fishless week is a rendezvous with the Hag of Misery. Seven men found themselves in the boot room, shedding waders and sharing dejection, their hands rounding the air about electric heaters as if in prayer. In the gloom, even Kells, who apparently preserved his prized lure yet another day and deployed it to advantage, could not exercise his glee. The men entered the lounge with sharp thirsts, to find a comfortable Torino, reading a magazine by the fire.

"You're in early." Beedle's voice was cool. He and Alexander were the only ones still speaking to the Ishmael.

"Yeah," Torino said. "It was awful out there. I quit before lunch."

"You mean your fly was out of the water?" Dorough asked incredulously.

"I offered it," Torino said, but Dorough turned and went to look for someone to drink with.

"Do any good?" Gib asked.

"Not really," Torino said.

By profession Beedle was trained to pursue evasion. "Did you catch any fish?"

"Not like yesterday," Torino dodged. "I got one, then hung it up."

"What size?" Alexander's voice reflected the effort he made to keep it flat.

"Oh, I don't know. Fair size."

They let that assessment stand until dinner. Keith MacPherson had guided Torino that day. He was asked at table about Joe's catch.

"A monster," said Keith, not given to praise. For marketing purposes Keith took a digital photo of every fish his guests netted. His camera made the rounds. There in the display was a classic brochure photo, a grinning, unshaven Torino gripping a cock salmon well north of twenty pounds.

Keith spoke of the fish proudly, as if he and not his Presbyterian Maker were responsible. "See the fierce kype on him." The male salmon develops a protruding jaw that hooks upwards. This bend was some five inches. The fish stretched in Tornino's hands, silver and black, awaiting its release.

"What's needed for the record?" Kells asked.

"Two more fish," Keith answered. "But he's lost his Green Lantern."

A hush settled over the group.

"Lost it? It broke off?"

"I must have dropped it," Torino said indifferently. "I stuck it in my hat, and when I got back to the lodge, it was gone."

"Ah, you poor bastard," said Dorough with evident glee. "Now you're as bad off as the rest of us." Someone reminded him that Kells was still fishing the magic fly. "Except Kells," Dorough allowed. "Unless of course a Green Lantern mysteriously appears. Unless whoever took that tinsel ties one in the middle of the night."

Torino looked at him with a face from which all expression had been drained.

The camera made the rounds. Men inspected the tiny screen in awe, and narrowed their eyes to look up at Torino's face, so excited in the photo, so calculatingly blank across the table. He was clearly masking his emotions. Further proof.

After dessert Gib passed a box of Monte Cristo #3s. Richard Rassenall tried to ease the tension with a recitation of "Casey at the Bat," complete with stagy gestures. The piece usually brought uproar, but tonight no one smiled. The men retired mindful of the morning, their last full day of fishing.

That night as he lay in bed, Gib Alexander regularly heard the soft footfalls of someone—was it more than one?—in the halls. He thought to investigate. Would indeed Torino sneak a round at Keith's tying vice? Would some of the men, many of them Gib's friends, ordinarily reasonable and peaceful, break into Torino's room and do him harm? He stayed where he was.

And in the morning Gib sat in front of a cooling English breakfast, too anxious to lift fork or spoon until all the chairs were occupied. Joe Torino was the last to arrive.

"Sleep well?" Gib asked.

"Like a baby," Joe answered and dug into a bowl of porridge.

Only later, in the boot room, was Gib able to corner Rassenall and find out what had caused the soft commotion in the halls.

"We took turns," Richard confessed. "I forget whose idea it was. Every half hour two of us roused ourselves. We wanted to catch him in the act, you see."

"Richard. I'm ashamed of you. And two men were necessary? Why? One to slip the noose over his head?"

For all his good humor Rassenall was not to be cowed into an apology. He had endured a long, cold week.

"A witness, you see. One man, he can deny it. But if two of us caught him in the act, why, we'd have him."

And so seven men, each accompanied by a stout Scot and each attired in heavy woolens, in oiled Barbour coats, in anoraks and hooded sweaters, set out for their final full day of sport. Torino stayed behind. He'd had, he said, enough.

Rassenall enlisted Mrs. Phillips to watch him like a hawk. "Let us know if he goes near Keith's tying bench."

"Ach, but there's none to mind if the man uses a bit of Keith's fur and feather."

"Just let us know, Mrs. Phillips. Let us know."

• • •

Three of them returned early because of the accident. In the icy rain, hands were cold and balance unsteady. Casting moments before lunch, no one catching anything and interest faint and distant as the Scottish sun, Leland Kells had slipped and gone in. How it happened, his ghillie said defensively, for it was a mark against the guide, he did not know. At one moment, the man was wading carefully towards the bank, to warm his legs in the air, staff firmly at his side, and in the next he was flailing about in the water.

"He floated right by me. I plucked him out like Moses from the reeds," the lad said, intending neither disrespect nor sacrilege. Kells had gotten a proper dunking, and before they brought him in, Dorough and Beedle insisted that he strip down in the car and wrap himself in a heavy Shetland blanket kept in the trunk for just this emergency. Still, the poor man who stumbled into the lodge had begun to shake, and his skin had turned the delicate blue of a Fabergé egg. Mrs. Phillips took charge, ordering him to a hot shower, putting on a large kettle, and collecting the soggy clothes from the car.

As tea was brewing, all the fisherman returned. The miserable conditions, the lack of the proper lure to catch whatever fish there were, and somehow the proximity of the Green Lanterns from London had underscored their futility. When news of Kells' mishap went up and down the river, they quickly availed themselves of a reason to quit.

They were sitting in the lounge. Mrs. Phillips was busy stirring up a quick shepherd's pie, the Macallan was well turned to hot toddies, and the group, save Torino in Coventry and Kells in the shower, was clustered together to commiserate on the sad ending of a sad week.

Mrs. Phillips entered with a tray.

"If you're truly chilled," she admonished them, "tea will warm you up."

"No better than whisky," said Rassenall.

"Aye, better. It's a medical fact," she said, and set the tray with its cups, saucers and teapot in their midst. "And when Mr. Kells joins you, please tell him I put his clothes in the wash. I'll have them dry for him if he wants to go out this afternoon."

That brought hoots of laughter. No one would leave the sanctuary of the lounge, now that they had shed their gear and warmed themselves by the fire.

"Oh, yes," she said and rummaged in her apron. "I took the liberty of emptying his pockets. You'll see that he gets these."

She put a handful of trinkets on the table. There was a lip balm, a nail clipper, a pair of reading glasses. And three spools of green tinsel.

Silence. The men stared at those spools as if they were the devil's teeth. Richard Rassenall spoke up. "I'll see that he gets them," he said to the long gone cook, and placed them in his pocket. No one said another word.

Nor did they when Torino, who had been in his room talking to his office by cell phone, joined them. He inquired about the day's catch, about what brought them back early, but there were few responses. Alexander told him briefly of Kells' slip, and explained that Mrs. Phillips was making them all lunch.

Neither Torino nor Kells came to table for the shepherd's pie. A girl from the kitchen served them a tray in their room. Kells for dinner too, and although Torino came and sat, there was no conversation of which he partook. Richard Rassenall recited from Burns' "Cutty Sark," but both he and his listeners had finished the single malt, so neither made much sense of it. Keith MacPherson distributed a few of the freshly arrived Lanterns and offered to tie more, but there seemed no appetite for them.

• • •

The next day the sun shone as brightly as it had the first. Joe Torino got up early, and took a long and stimulating walk into town and back. He shopped for his wife and children, buying souvenir tams and packaged shortbread. A few of the men had taken their catch to the smokehouse, and they drove to pick up their fish, packed expertly in dry ice for the flight back.

Those who fished went empty-handed—the weather was too bright for catching. "All occasion," Rassenall quoted Macbeth to them of the week's fortunes. "'All occasion doth conspire against me and spurs on my dull revenge.'"

A minibus drove them to the Aberdeen airport where they would divide into the first fractions. Some would fly to Gatwick, others Heathrow, one had a connection through Dublin. They said their good-byes outside the duty-free shop.

"Not many fish," Rassenall said, shaking Gib's hand enthusiastically. "But an experience. Life is full of experiences."

The Robards brothers asked Gib where he planned their next trip. They talked of the Kharlovka, the Litza, the Deschuttes, the Grand Cascope. Someone mentioned Iceland, the Grisma, or the Big Laxa. Torino was off pricing perfumes and aftershave. Six men gathered about, and someone waved Leland Kells into the huddle.

"Iceland," one of the Robardses said, his arm linking with that of Kells'. "Iceland would be exciting. Beautiful place, good sport. But, Gib, if I may? I'd suggest perhaps a smaller group?"

PACKING IT IN

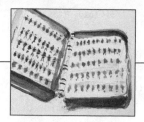

FOR THE
SPORT OF IT

When Prescott Demarest travels in the sporting world, he is treated with a deference that all but meets the measure of his expectations. Grouse lodges in Scotland, boatmen on the Yellowstone, even lowly birding guides from the Chirachuas to Prince Edward Island recognize his name and grow timorous in his presence. You recognize it too, the several books with full color plates on upland game, the regular and monitory columns in that magazine, the two-volume work on Atlantic salmon. His reputation and his encyclopedic knowledge about the outdoors are known virtually throughout the world.

Virtually.

In Marcallo Cay, they catch a lot of bonefish and snook. For thirty years the world record for permit on a fly was held by someone who landed and released a fish on Marcallo's flats.

They catch fish, but they don't read much. So when Prescott's secretary booked his trip to Marcallo, spoke his name to the lodge owner and awaited the reverential hush, she was disappointed. Ezekiel

Roland expressed neither surprise nor awe. He simply confirmed two rooms for two couples, three days and three nights.

The secretary knew her boss's standards, and was already skeptical when she could find Horseshoe Crab Lodge in none of her directories. When the owner himself seemed unaware of the reputation of Mr. Demarest, she reported her concerns. Mr. Demarest waived them all: wonderful to find a modest little place. We'll spread the gospel, educate the natives. A chance to get away.

The smudged brochure that arrived the next week tended to firm up her guess. Hot water at midday only, rates that hadn't been revised since World War II, a one-story cinder-block house for bed and a second, identical house for board. No swimming pool, no boating, no fly shop. No amenities, period. Get away, Mr. D had said. Getting away to most people meant getting away from their gripes. But luxury and celebrity never annoyed Prescott Demarest; they sustained him. Was this what he really wanted?

Ann Demarest handled the flyleaf by its one clean corner and asked the same question. She considered sending it on to the Campbells, but—blurred, unfiltered photographs on grainy paper—it looked too dreary. Mimi Campbell had reluctantly agreed to come along to keep her company, and Ann didn't want her backing out. Neither of the women cared about fishing. Her husband George liked the occasional outing. Fishing, he said for the sole purpose of nettling Demarest, seemed like a pointless pursuit. He had never caught bonefish, he told them, but he would be happy to try. In the bottom drawer of his bureau, George had a safari outfit that Mimi would not let him wear in Central Park. This would be its chance. So long as Prescott didn't mind putting up with an amateur.

Of course Prescott minded. But he wanted to show his friends this part of the world, to take that smug George Campbell down a peg or two, and to demonstrate, with long, delicate casts that resembled French curves, a mastery of the subject. So he grudgingly consented.

On a spring Friday, the two couples flew from LaGuardia to Nassau. Ann and the Campbells hit the casinos. Prescott stayed in his room, tying Bimini bights, honing the points of flies, oiling the reels. The flight to Marcallo Cay left at dawn. They would touch down in time for a full day of fishing.

The De Havilland Otter departed Nassau on time. The four sat two abreast, the women at the window seats so they could admire the palette of colors as it passed beneath them. Their route took them down the far coast of Andros, over Staniel Cay and Crooked Island. The water changed from blue to blue to blue. The plane's shadow skimmed the turquoise surface, and looking down from separate windows Ann and Mimi imagined the same dream, schools of fish, schools of darting fish, and mused on the name Prescott had told them that was given to this part of the sea: the Tongue of the Ocean. Random bars of land rose in the shallows, their edges traced perfectly by fringes of green. Exquisite embroidery, trimmed here and there in creamy white.

Prescott interrupted Ann's reverie. His voice might have been the sound track of a travelogue.

"This population is mostly uneducated, little employment. The produce is meager, because the soil is so thin. And there are few beaches," he went on. "Most of the Bahamian island mass is uninhabitable, swamp."

Prescott used the lesson for more than geography. He let down the tray in front of him, pulled three fly boxes from his traveling bag. Leaned across the aisle and tapped the arm of George Campbell.

"You'll need to know your patterns," he began. "See here. This entire box is bonefish. One finds it useful to classify them by sink rate. Sink rate in turn depends on a number of factors including salinity. You'll notice the top row appears to be the same, Crazy Charlies, but by varying the amount of lead wire tied onto the hook one can vary the sink rate. If one wishes." Prescott often spoke, as he wrote, in the third person. On occasion he became stuck there, like a sedan in a soft shoulder, until an editor towed him out.

George looked across and feigned interest. By the last box, Deceivers and Glass Minnows, he had forgotten what it was that Prescott meant him to know.

Behind them, Prescott noticed a young black man who seemed to be listening in. He turned with a smile.

"Bonefishing," Prescott said precisely, so the man might grasp what he was saying. "Do you know bonefishing?"

"Yes, mister."

"And these," he said, reaching for a fourth box and opening its lid. "These are for permit and tarpon. Did you know these waters hold permit and tarpon?"

"Yes, mister."

Satisfied, Prescott turned back. George was reaching into the seat pocket for the in-flight magazine, but a quick word blocked his path to sanctuary.

"George? See here. For leaders . . .

"We're going backwards, from fly to the reel and rod, but it will do. One should really learn these the other way. Leaders attach the fly to the fly line. I've made up a batch for us." He took out a slender wallet. Ten leaders lay within, each coiled and held in place by a wire twist. "I use four feet of twenty-five pound, three feet of twenty pound, two feet of fifteen pound, and a foot of twelve pound. That gives me ten feet. If one needs more because of, say, bright sun, one simply adds tippet. You'll notice that I've used surgeon's loops here, but when you come to add tippet, you had better learn the Bimini twist. We'll learn those tonight at dinner."

Prescott looked back to the young man behind him. "Knots," he said loudly. The man nodded. Campbell made a futile attempt to involve himself in the women's conversation, but there was none. Prescott collected him on the rebound.

"Now if one gets a shot at barracuda, one wants these." A different wallet. "They're wire, and the gauge one uses will depend on the wind and how well he is getting the line out. One needs time to practice casting. Without the double haul, it's no use. I don't know what we'll do with the ladies."

It was a short flight, a stop at Congo Town then on south to Marcallo. The wheels touched down as Prescott was reviewing the proper way to thread the backing over the reel. He had several subjects left.

The airstrip was a slab of asphalt cut into the scrub. Three large and handsome women disembarked first, followed by the khaki-clad fisherfolk, and finally the young man from the rearmost row. All eight passengers waited together on the broken pitch as the pilot opened the forward hatch and took out their luggage. Prescott's pieces, forest green canvas with leather trim, came together easily. His several rods for varying conditions were fitted into a matching rod case. The secretary had arranged that; for the three others, the lodge would provide tackle.

Each of the returning women was met by an eager husband, and the reunited couples lined up to board a bus. Beyond the hurricane fence was parked one other vehicle, an unlikely VW van, its original maroon now piebald with rust. The driver stayed coolly inside, until the Campbells and the Demarests approached. Then he hopped out.

"How do you do, Ladies and Gentlemen." The man was short and clearly fit. His age was indeterminable, the clues inconclusive. His hair, uniformly and sable gray, curled tight against his scalp, and his bright face, several shades of aubergine and equally shiny, had not a single line. Bulbous gold molars flashed sunlight when he smiled. Around his neck he wore a length of bead chains assembled from key rings, and from the chain hung a stone cross the size of a grenade.

"How do you do? You are the Campbells and the Demarests come all the way from New York City for some sport fishing. I will be your host and one of your guides, for I am Mr. Roland."

All four shook his hand.

"And this," they turned to find the quiet young man from the plane, again behind them, "this will be your other guide. Mr. Roland."

"I thought," said Ann, "that you were Mr. Roland."

"You are to be congratulated as a close listener, lady." His gold and ivory smile gleamed. "I am Mr. Ezekiel Roland," his voice rose with the delight of his punchline. "And this is Mr. Roland Roland." With that he gave out an infectious laugh that sounded over the firing of the De Havilland's rotary engines.

"He is," Mr. Ezekiel explained the joke, "my nephew."

They piled into the van and began the bumpy and serpentine trip to the lodge. Serpentine because, for every pedestrian or housewife hanging the wash, for every cyclist or bean-row hoer or step-sitter, Mr. Ezekiel Roland swerved to that side of the road and called out the news. "The sterilizer arrived on the flight, Mrs. Beasely-Brown." "The day will be warm, Solomon, but squalls in the afternoon." "Your book is overdue at the library, young Roland. Five cents a day."

"That is our church," he shouted proudly. "The A. M. E. Shorter." They looked quickly to see a Quonset hut fly by, a magnetic letter sign in front quoting from the gospel of Luke. "And that is the Second Marcallo Abyssinian Baptist," this a small aqua building that traveled past the van at the same speed, boards over its two windows.

"What became of the First Marcallo Abyssinian Baptist?" Mimi asked.

"Blown away," said Ezekiel Roland. "First in '82 by Michael, then in '94 by Isaiah, and finally last year. A little squall, unnamed, not even a prophet. I preach that these events may manifest God's suggestion to the good people of the congregation that they consider joining the A. M. E. Shorter."

Again the laugh, piercing and infectious. Everyone but Prescott joined in.

"You preach, Mr. Roland?"

"I do, lady. I preach the gospel of our Lord Jesus Christ every Sunday. To the willing and the napping alike."

"In addition to running the lodge?"

"Oh yes. The Lord has several tasks for me. I am the island librarian, my family runs the bottled water plant and the liquor store, we can stop to allow you to stock up. And I own a boat yard."

"A boat yard," Ann repeated.

"Hull repairs, lady. Mostly I send engines on to Nassau. Every so often, the Lord sends me a motor for which in His wisdom He has also sent me the part."

"You should ask the Lord for a larger inventory."

"Yes, yes," Ezekiel greatly liked the idea and flashed his noon-gold smile. "But then the Lord must look after the people in Nassau too."

The lodge was no grander than advertised. The two main buildings were painted Kelly green with blue shutters. The guesthouse had a small sitting area, an adequate bathroom, and two bedrooms where window air conditioners roared mightily and produced, in place of cool air, a steady drip of water into two aluminum cookie pans beneath. Surrounding the complex a mortared wall was sloughing off its coat of pink paint. At Prescott's urging, they unpacked quickly. He was resolute to make the most of their three days.

Faced with no possible alternate activity, the women decided to come along.

"It's not like sitting on a dock," Prescott warned. "If one can't get the fly out at least forty feet into a ten-knot breeze, one needn't bother."

But they bothered. On the first day, the Demarests were guided by Roland Roland and the Campbells by Ezekial. It would be a short trip, the elder Roland explained. Back at six for dinner or Cook would be unhappy. They would go to nearby flats and see how their luck ran.

The boats spun out over the seas. While there were few waves, there were regular swells, and with the engines at full throttle the passengers rode as if perched on a jackhammer. In the pouncing boat, Prescott had all he could do to hold on. Finally, on a smooth patch, he pulled from his pocket a palm-sized book of tables.

"When is your high tide?" he called to Roland Roland.

"Depends," Roland shouted back. "Winds, moon . . ."

"Of course," Prescott said. "I understand that. I mean today. When is your high tide today?"

"About an hour ago."

"Aha," Prescott said to no one in particular. "Tide going out. It should be a neap tide, we're in the third quarter." He poked Ann to make sure she was listening. "For seven days the moon is closer to us than at any time in the month. The sun and moon are in a near direct line. The corresponding positions increase gravitational pull. Those are spring tides, and one says the moon is in perigee." He pointed to the book in his hand, though at what Ann didn't know.

"As the moon continues to orbit the earth, there will only be a slight rise and fall in tide for the next seven-day period. That's a neap tide. They're lower. We're here during a neap tide."

"Good or bad?"

"It's not so simple as good or bad. One must calculate one's position accordingly. A neap tide where there's a northerly wind, and we're an hour past peak. I'm going to fish the leeward side of the flats. That's where the fish will be."

"Windward," said Roland Roland.

"What?"

"Windward."

Demarest let escape a sly smile. He looked at his wife sympathetically.

"Tell me, Roland. Do you also work in the family water business?"

"I do."

"And at the boat yard?"

"I do. Also I run the gas station up north."

"I see. Well, you should understand. This is my only business. I'm thought to be rather good at it. My business is to know where the fish are."

"You are a bonefish guide?"

"I am Prescott Demarest. The writer. Have you never heard of me?"

"Oh no, mister. I heard. You made the reservations."

The boat slowed, Prescott looked up. Ahead, Ezekial's boat had also throttled down as it approached a thin line of mangrove keys.

"This is perfect," Prescott said. "I'll get out here and wade."

"No," said Roland. "Fish from the boat. The bottom . . ."

"Nonsense. I always wade. It's not bonefishing if you don't wade. The bottom is quite adequate."

"Not for walking. Besides the fish are on the other side."

"My dear fellow." Despite the rocking skiff, Prescott pulled himself up to full height. "You don't seem to recognize a master of the subject." And he gave a grimacing smile he meant to be dismissive. With that he removed his rod from the boat's rack, pulled his long-billed cap tight to his brow, and swung his legs over the side. He took particular delight in the cap. It had flaps to keep the sun off one's neck and his own signature embroidered on the side. Roland cut the engine, and Prescott let himself down into the thigh-deep water.

"Do remind him, dear," he called to his wife. "Pick me up. They can be forgetful." Ann waved cheerfully, and Roland took the boat to the north side of the keys.

Prescott had tough going. Twice he was sure he saw feeding bonefish, but by the time he slogged the forty or fifty yards to the site, they were gone. Every so often he came upon a lethargic ray, and in frustration cast his fly to it. Swells and crabholes had refigured the sand with pitch and pothole, and more than once Demarest went in over his head.

The sun lengthened its light as it sunk into a lavender sky. Far off a squall built and sailed by. It was a spectacular horizon, the kind only a postcard could show without self-consciousness.

On the other side of the mangroves, the two boats poled slowly across the shoreline until they met up with fish. There seemed to be three distinct schools. At first, each looked like a patch of saw grass, gray and dancing against the bottom. But the patch migrated slowly as the bone snuffled for crab. Any harsh movement, the clank of pole against boat, Mimi dropping her rod, sent a nervous and silver shiver through the school, but the pack never bolted.

The fishing was easy. The guides poled them upwind of the schools, and, even though new to the motion, they found if they got a back cast high into the air, the wind delivered them a perfect cast. They fished mostly from the boat, and got out to wade for the fun of it. No one went more than five minutes without a fish on. Once a black-tipped shark came to feed amongst the schools, and guests and guides re-boarded and watched him swim lazily through, striking with fierce alacrity but not always with success. Beyond their target, a barracuda chased a swarm of shiners, and the little fish rained out of the water like dimes flipped from a skillet.

Dinner had a somber bass note. The Campbells and Ann Demarest were keen converts to the sport. They recounted for Prescott memorable catches. Each had boated over a dozen bonefish, and hooked almost as many again where the fly had been thrown or the fish had cannily run to the mangroves and broken them off. They were so flushed with their sport they didn't notice the set of Demarest's jaw.

"Perhaps," he said as the last of the grouper, peas from a can, and buttered potatoes were downed, "perhaps tomorrow we should switch around. Ann and I will go out with Ezekiel."

And that is what they did. Outbound, Prescott took the opportunity of correcting the owner on his business concept.

"This lodge isn't viable, man. Two rooms aren't enough. You need enough density to advertise. Start with a small classified in the better fishing magazines. That will generate extra revenues, which you can then use to build another few units. Soon you'll be able to move to a display ad."

Ezekiel said nothing, simply kept his eye on the seas as the two boats set out for a more distant location. This day they were headed to a tiny archipelago. The locals called it the airport, ever since a single-engine Piper ditched in its shallows for a drug drop. The cannibalized airplane happened to mark the site of crab fields that brought in the bones.

"Now," continued Prescott as the boat bounced along, "once you've upscaled the physical plant, you'll need to do something about the kitchen. That fat woman seems very nice, but she overcooks the fish. A better clientele will want a more sophisticated touch."

Ezekiel nodded and said nothing. They arrived before the tide peaked. Prescott studied the winds and the tides and again decided to stake himself out far from the boats, this time on the western tip of the islands.

"The fish not here, mister." Ezekiel was eager for all his guests to enjoy themselves, even Prescott. "The fish down below."

"They'll be running this way," Prescott said. "Do you know that NOAA employs thirty-seven factors in making tidal predictions?"

"NOAA?"

"The National Oceanic and Atmospheric Administration."

Their table that night was gloomy. Ann and the Campbells assembled before Prescott arrived and told their tales of screaming reels and sly takes. Joined as a foursome, Ann changed the talk to maintenance fees for New York co-ops. After dinner, concerned that Prescott's words might have gotten back to the cook, Ann mentioned to her how delicious the dinner was.

"You don't need to worry about keeping your job," she said with tact.

"Oh, I don't worry, lady." She gave a familiar burst of maniacal laughter. "Ezekiel, he's my husband."

Prescott didn't stay for the lemon curd cake. In one sense that was a pity since it was delicious. In a second, it was a blessing: Ann wanted to tell the story of the eight-pounder she had landed on her own.

On the last day Prescott relented. He would stand where he was put, and fish how he was told. The boats went off to a third destination.

For hours Ezekiel and Roland poled their guests through the flats. In the morning the sun beat hard on them, and the water was clear. But the fishing gods can be as fickle and perverse as their mortal imitators. There were few fish. By chance—unless you ascribe to those gods, as some do, a mordant sense of humor—when the morning singles passed, George Campbell was on the deck of Ezekiel's boat, not Prescott. A building breeze came at them, and as a neophyte George was able to get his cast out to reach only two. He pulled both of them in. On Prescott's watch, the seas were bare.

"Don't worry," said George, in a genuine but vain attempt to cheer his companion. "You know what they say. Plenty of fish in the ocean."

The boats pulled gunnels to gunnels for the picnic lunch. Prescott wore his dark cloud of failure like a halo. A south wind rose and the surface dimpled, obscuring any trace of feeding bone beneath it.

"May be an early day," ventured Roland Roland.

"Now listen, young man. I'm not leaving 'til I catch a fish."

"No one can catch fish in this," George said, more of a question. "You won't be able to get your cast out."

"You too?" Prescott said through tight lips. He leaped to the bow, loosed some line, and began to crank out an angry line. A double-hauled speed cast went thirty yards into the teeth of the wind.

"Very nice," said Roland. "That would catch Mister Fish. If Mister Fish was there."

After lunch the boats traced the shoreline. Only Prescott fished, grunting now with each cast. They came to a channel in the islands, where a ten-foot gap parted the mangroves. Roland pulled his boat alongside his uncle's.

"There," he said to Prescott pointing to the gap. "Can you get your line through there?"

"Absolutely."

"There's a nice fish working on the other side. Just lay your fly through there. Keep at it."

Prescott took the bow and began his false casts. He was concentrating with such diligence he failed to see Roland's boat motor off. It would be quite a feat, he knew, but all eyes were on him and he sucked resolve into the back cast and let go. He knew how to handle a rod. The fly went through the gap and out the other side.

"Now," said Ezekiel. "Begin the retrieve."

Prescott stripped his line in, varying the speed and length of each pull. He squinted into the wind and prayed. This fish would be enough. One fish, let him get one. The first cast took nothing, nor the second. Ezekiel encouraged him.

"You are on the mark, mister. Do it again."

By now Roland's boat, carrying the two puzzled women, had rounded the island and made the far side of the gap. Roland slipped anchor and picked up a rod. When Prescott's fly came whistling through the mangroves and splashed to the water, Roland watched it sink. Then he let go his own cast, right on top.

Prescott felt the tug. The sublime, miraculous tug. "Fish," he whispered reverentially.

"Fish," Ezekiel whispered back. "Careful."

Prescott raised the rod tip and struck. The line reacted as he expected—it ran. And what a run. Prescott was into his backing in seconds. When the run stopped, he recovered ground, hoping to get a look at his prize. But just as he brought the line in, just where the gap was, the fish made a second, heroic run. This time Prescott feared his backing wouldn't be sufficient—he called to George to witness one hundred yards of backing down to the last few loops. His heart pounded as he felt the fish tire, and he began to haul him in. Then, astonishingly,

again just as he thought he might get a glimpse of the fish, it ran. A
third time, fifteen minutes into the fight. Ran headstrong without a
pause, giving its pursuer no chance to turn it. Prescott watched in rap-
ture, in horror as the last helix of Dacron spun off. The Duncan loop
that he had tied to secure the backing to the reel gave with a pop. Fly,
leader, line and backing disappeared into the Caribbean like a Carnival
snake.

Limp from the fight, Prescott staggered back to his chair.

"My God," he said.

"That some fish," Ezekiel said.

"My God," Prescott said again.

"Too bad," George consoled.

"What do you think, Ezekiel? How big was that fish?"

"Hard to say, Mister. He was the grand daddy."

"He was, wasn't he? The grand daddy of bone."

"The grand daddy," Ezekiel said and let go one of his steam engine
laughs.

"I wonder what the record for a bonefish on a fly is," Prescott
mused. "I wonder if that wouldn't have done it."

Roland poled his boat up.

"Some fight."

"The grand daddy," George told him. "Prescott hooked the grand
daddy of bone."

Both women looked on admiringly.

That evening was festive. Prescott mixed his famous Jamaican rum
punch. He was even prepared to steam the rock lobster, he knew a
special recipe with sherry, but Ann prevailed on him to stand down.
The cook might be insulted, she said.

• • •

Back in the city, Prescott told the story of the fight often. He told of
the feral pull, the heart that powered three runs, the flash of meaty silver

that he estimated at two and a half feet in length. At some of these dinner parties there was a fisherman, and even if there weren't the story
had, he felt, universal interest. He considered writing it up. He even had
a title: "The Grand Daddy." Somehow, the tale summed up fly fishing
for the sport of it.

Ann argued against doing a story. Prescott rarely took her advice
on professional matters, they were after all his province. She persisted.
Better, she said, to keep the memory of it to yourself. That persuaded
him—she was right.

MOTHER'S DAY

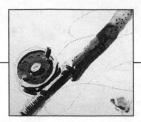

I CAN PROVE IT

You may find this hard to believe, but I have proof.

It was the first day of the season. I catalogued my gear as I stowed it into the back of the SUV. Rod, reel, net, flies. Man against fish. Streamer wallet, nymph boxes by size and color, weight, line dressing. The primordial battle. Fly floatant, leader sink, line indicators. Wit against instinct. Tippet spools, sinking line, forceps, stomach pump, thermometer. Almost as an afterthought, a camera.

I was heading to a stream, only two hours from Denver, that trickles out of a high artesian ridge in the Rockies, so obscure it has no name. I've taken friends there, but not many. Most object to the blindfolds, the affidavits, the subsequent deprogramming sessions and hypnosis.

And so this day I set off alone. The sky was full of promise and blue, the blue of a Monet landscape. At last I pulled the car into a grove of aspen, turned off the engine and sighed.

Could it be Manet?

Within minutes I'd tied into the first fish of the day. Brookies packed the stream, and after the long winter they were carnivorous. These were not big fish, but they were manly fish.

At noon I stopped to nap. When I awoke, there was an eerie silence. Before my nap the stream had been pocked with rising fish, the air had filled with the sounds of their splashing. Now it was as if Nature herself was waiting, or maybe Roy Scheider and Richard Dreyfuss. I studied the stream. A tiny calibaetis hatch was on, a fly no larger than a dust mote. Most fishermen would have missed it, and of the rest, few would have thought it worth trying. For me it was the ultimate challenge: to replicate the unique.

I searched my several boxes but could find nothing similar. There was only one answer. I retrieved my streamside vice from deep within my vest and clamped the jaws on a hook. It had been specially forged for me in a foundry in southern Sweden, a size thirty-eight barbless. For a tail, I tied in a hair that I'd plucked for just this purpose from the second finger joint of a Turkish consul who'd dozed off one night after dinner. The hackle was less dun than opal.

Finally the dubbing. Years ago I'd been given a pelt as a gift, a re-membrance. Libel laws and my own sense of chivalry prevent record-ing the lady's name. The pelt came from a fox raised in a monastery in Breton, fed only on newborn chicks and mocha almond torte. This was a fox that had never even dated. From the belly I clipped a whisper of fur, and, removing the guard hairs, spun it on. The fly had barely been finished when a male calibaetis, dashing from the water's edge, not only tried to mate with it, but succeeded, retreating with a smile. The final test was still ahead.

Ready at last. I walked upstream, past a gate of two boulders through which the water coursed with a fury. Thirty, maybe forty yards up, was the spot. The stream bent at a right angle. At the elbow the current formed a cutbank and in its elbow a deep hole.

The surface was guarded by willow and scrub oak. There was a band of water, perhaps four inches across, where a fly could float without a snag. The overhang wasn't the problem, though. This inviting lie could be reached only with a cast across two currents, one swift and constant, the second a subtler current drifting towards the far bank.

As I sat contemplating the problem, I saw a rise that stopped my heart. A sip dimpled the pool, a sip so slight I wasn't sure it had happened. A touch of lips, gentler than a blink.

Slowly, holding my breath, I rose and stood on tip-toes. There under the surface—could I be sure?—was an enormous shape, blacker than night, un-piscatorial, and yet from its motion, clearly a trout.

I knew then what must be done. There would only be one chance at the fish, and only one cast that could reach him. I'd tried it before as a lark, one slow day in the Pyrenees. It begins with an ordinary motion, but as the power stroke ends, you manipulate your forearm and wrist in opposite, or more accurately obverse, directions. The technique cannot be described, which is why it is rarely executed. It is a combination of the S cast and the Patagonian J, but in fact the line falls to the water in the form of the mystical Hebrew letter Tsadde.

I let out line. Distance was not a problem—I've been known to cast one hundred feet without a rod, fifty without line. One false cast to get airborne and . . . voilà. Coils fell to the water. Currents dissipated the slack, the fly sat briefly among the willows, and when it disappeared I struck.

To what happened next, I cannot swear. There was an unearthly scream of gear on gear, a race upstream, leaps beyond the azimuth of the sun. Half an hour passed in a heartbeat. As the fight was ending, we headed downstream. I realized that, should the giant fish pass through the boulder gate at the bottom of the pool, he'd be lost.

So, just as we approached the opening, I horsed his head upstream. And he stuck.

Exhausted from the fight, this magnificent trout turned broadside to the current and became lodged in the boulders. The pressure of the water held him fast.

I couldn't believe my fortune. Dropping my rod on the bank, I ran for the camera. Only after I'd set up the tripod, read the meter, and chosen an exposure did I realize my peril: the body of the fish had blocked the outlet, and the water was rising. I hastily snapped the shutter, and by then water had risen chest-high. Desperately I made for shore. Even as I sloshed in panic, the shoreline receded from me as a reservoir filled the meadow. Exhausted and humming "Eternal Father Strong to Save," I leaped at an overhanging branch, swung myself out, and fell to dry land. The line, taut against the fish, snapped as I fell on it.

And so the fish escaped, the water subsided. Within minutes the stream returned to its banks.

• • •

It's not a story I like to tell. Many are skeptical, I can see it in their eyes. The photograph is inconclusive, the lens left unfocused in my rush to save my life. I have only the conviction, the knowledge as if revealed, that it happened. That, and one scrap of hard proof. For while you can't tell from the snapshot whether it's a fish or a rock, the print itself weighs seven pounds.

THE VETERAN

THE TARPON
OFF THE WALL

"It's always been out of place, darling."

He perched on the top step of the ladder, balancing himself with the mounted fish. She spoke the words with her back to him.

"A fish out of water."

"Out of place how?" He stood unsure what to do. Her voice was soft and tired, as if she'd said these very thoughts often.

"Out of place with the rest of the room." He looked about. He hadn't noticed until now. The room was furnished in a light chintz print, creams and lavenders. The writing desk was Queen Anne, the liquor cabinet an early Connecticut hanging cupboard.

"It's a den, Louise. It's where you would put a tarpon."

"Is that what it is? I wonder why I repress the word. Perhaps because it sounds a bit sinister, like a feminine hygiene product."

Henry descended the three steps balancing the plaque and placed it behind his cartons. Of the three clusters of boxes, his was the smallest.

Louise let out a sigh. "If only you'd taken up bridge."

"Where would you prefer to have a fish if not in the den?"

Louise was inspecting a chinoiserie lacquer tray. "I'm sorry, darling?" He repeated his question.

"I would prefer to have it in a skillet. Au burre blanc. If I must have it in the house at all."

She went on quickly. "This came from those odd friends of your parents. For our wedding? the man who wore the white belt? I think it's Bengali."

"Yours by all means. If you want it." Henry knew her intentions from the inflection of her voice, the slight retreat of her head while she regarded the tray. He hadn't been wrong yet. She placed the inlaid tray by the carton with the demitasse cups. Most of what had been in the breakfront, indeed most of the appointments of the room, sat in her cartons.

"We're not doing our share for dear old St. James," she said cheerfully as she approached the far bookcase. The books were mostly his. One by one she read off titles and he indicated his stack or that of St. James. Louise's church, or so Henry considered it.

"He won't mind. He was martyred. Arrows I think."

"Killed by a mob."

"Still. Doesn't leave much time for reading."

"How about these, darling?" Louise's choice of the word was prompted not by affection but by a disinclination towards his Christian name. She had never liked it, and particularly now, with the marriage all but dissolved save the court order, she felt that its use would signal a certain intimacy. Henry squinted. Louise was holding up tattered copies of The Iliad and The Odyssey.

"I've had those since college days."

"Exactly."

"No. I want to keep them. Someday I'll reread them."

She shrugged at the news and tossed the books without malice into a near carton.

"While you're up there, let me hand you a cloth. You can give those moldings a once-over."

He wasn't up there. She found a dust rag and he remounted the ladder. She continued to read titles as he worked. Every so often, when her tone betokened that he was lacking in charity, he would cede a book to St. James. And, gratified, she would walk to the cartons by the door and place the volume on a neat pile.

He turned the cloth inside out. "It's curious. This house doesn't signify me at all. There's the mounted tarpon and that's it."

"Your books," she said.

"And my books. But my fly rods are in the basement, my shot-guns and skis in the garage. Did you ever notice, Louise, that with a few strokes we have eliminated any evidence that I ever lived here?"

"Now, now. No need to get morbid." They continued their tasks in silence. Occasionally she would call out a title and he would decide.

She opened the china cabinet and began winding bubble wrap about her Rosenthal plates. "Besides, the realtor says the house will show better with our things out of it. Did I tell you he's going to repaint all the walls before he puts it on the market? An off-white."

At last, Henry said, but to himself. He watched her consider small pieces—the bell they had never liked, the silver sugar basket. She was stingier to the church than he had been. On the top row were special pieces, beyond the pull, he felt sure, of her conscience: her mother's cordial set, the commemorative plates, and the ivory netsuke he had bought for her on their trip to Japan. It was, they had been told, a fer-tility symbol.

"Why in the world would you keep that fish?" Its glassy eye had arrested her as she made her way about the room.

"I don't know. That was a great week, a special fish."

She let it pass. He decided on a last phrase.

"Happier times."

"You prefer the company of men, darling. You should admit that about yourself. Nothing shameful. Not necessarily homoerotic." He promised himself he would not take the bait. "Now you'll have ample time for those trips."

He finished the moldings. Anticipating her next move, he slid the ladder over to the doorjamb, climbed up, and resumed dusting.

"The men from St. James will be here any moment. If you have something in the bedroom for them, you might pack it as well."

"They don't want my underwear, do they?"

"Anything at all. You might just take a look, I'd hate to call them back."

He descended, folded the dust cloth and lay it on the ladder step, and went to see what he could find. The sight of his old, familiar clothes saddened him. He decided to give some things away. A few sweaters, ties Louise had found too young for him, shirts he'd tired of. At the rear of the top drawer was a dress set. A present from Louise. He opened the velvet box. The cuff links were oversized and had to be forced through the buttonholes, so that whenever he put on a tuxedo they made him late. Or at the very least irritable.

When they had agreed on the divorce, she said that life was like a closet. When you cleared out old things, you made room for new ones. He couldn't remember now how the divorce had come about. She suggested a time apart. Once they began dividing furniture, the rest followed.

The dress set was expensive, each piece faced in lapis and centered with a diamond chip. Whenever he wore the set, he found himself looking down his shirtfront and thinking of a casino ship floating beyond the three-mile limit. He closed the lid and slipped the box into his pocket.

"Any luck?"

"More than I would have guessed." He placed the clothing in a half-filled carton marked for the church and tucked the dress set underneath. His hand hit against an object, and he peeked in to see. It was the netsuke.

"That will be the men from St. James. Darling, do go see if there's beer in the refrigerator. I should offer them something."

Henry obliged. If he lingered long enough he would miss the inevitable offer of his help to load their truck.

"I'm afraid I don't have that much for you," Louise said to the two volunteers. "There's the love seat and hassock, and those boxes."

The men carried the furniture into their truck. They returned with a dolly to fetch the boxes.

"That's it?" They stood by the cartons in the bare room. The shelves were clean and empty and the wood floor glistened.

Louise eyed a dust ball as if it were a rodent. On the wall she saw an outline where the fish had hung. She knew Henry was skulking in the back of the house, probably had turned on her kitchen television to watch some game.

"Not quite," she said. "Here, take this too." They loaded the dolly. It was fitted with a strap and winch, so they managed all the boxes in a single trip. They left. One man pushed the dolly, and under his arm the second carried the plaque Louise had given him, tarpon side out.

DOWNPOUR

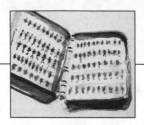

WHAT HE SEES

What he sees when he stands in the stream has nothing to do with fish or fishing. He no longer looks for trout—he's been at it so long, he carries an expectation of where the trout will gather. When they do appear it is as movement and shadow, and by then it's too late. Nor does he look at the rigging—a blue-winged olive floats ahead and his eyes follow it merely as the reminder of his original and now dimmed intention. It might be a bookmark he has put between pages awaiting his return.

He sees himself with wings. Two teals, duck and drake, have dropped themselves down in the pool above, and have begun to munch and nuzzle in the floating cress. He watched them land, how they gathered in the air by cupping the axillary feathers, holding on to the air and gripping themselves into a perfect stall inches from the water's surface. Not a splash.

The breeze moves behind him and his line slaps the water. The ducks look up, see him for the first time, and scurry. Compared to the greased landing, their takeoff is a clumsy flutter. They stretch themselves and run on the water, then flap madly to produce lift. Once airborne their wings flag heavily. They are not the bird he imagines for himself. Perhaps a hawk. A red-tail, imperious and alone. An eagle is too conspicuous, too elaborate, it takes constant feeding to keep itself aloft. Better a peregrine, sleek and efficient, or his friend the osprey, who occasionally fishes overhead.

Again the wind shifts; this time a strong gust scallops the water's surface. What if wind were tinted, what if you could choose one of those little rectangles of watercolor that come in the black tin, and fill in each breeze? How the gentian violet would mix with the pink, how mauve would bleed into the Prussian blue. The colors of sleep.

The moving air carries a scent to him, a scent of pine needle and stone. Ahead the rock of the cliff shines from a quick morning rain, and the breeze that bends off it brings a basal smell. As if the earth were freshly made. He casts the baetis imitation into the seam of two currents running together and senses interest. A pass. Is the fly too large? Should he change? He fishes the seam on both lips. The fly enters the center of the slip and goes under, but from the force of the water, not from a fish. He moves the fly fast in the air to dry it.

The scent puts him in mind of an excellent cigar. He thinks on that aroma, a cigar on the bank while waiting for the hatch to appear. The thought is a sweet one, as much temptation as these days he can tolerate. He sees the smoke and feels the smell in his nostrils, that and the aroma of a browned turkey fresh from the oven. Why the two he can't explain, where the turkey has come from, but they come together. Now he sees the turkey, a presentation from some past feast; he sees the parsley and nestled by it roast yams, all on a thick china platter.

The past is easy to see. It stands just beyond the horizon—he looks up at the horizon and the land begins to float. The stream stays fixed, only the water moves, and the horizon floats away like a stage set, as if to give him a view of what's behind it.

What is behind the past? Is that where the future lies stored? If he were given the chance, would he choose to see the future? Would he rather read minds, be invisible?

No value in seeing the future. Oh, he could pick up the newspaper and peek at the stock quotes, but all that would get him was money. Nothing wrong with money, though at the moment it seems prodigal, unneeded, a sack of pebbles. Anyone who sees the future will know whether a fish is waiting for the blue-winged olive, will know how that fish will take it and where he'll run. Not for him. What about reading minds? What would that tell you that you couldn't otherwise find out? It might have been useful when he'd pursued success or women, but those were a young mug's games.

And invisibility? Somehow he didn't want to surrender any of the senses. Just the opposite.

He has waded up from the seam where the currents braided, and the fly now drifts easily. He steps onto a flat headed by an anvil-shaped rock that shelters water as it comes at him. The fly floats long and straight without drag. If he were invisible, he would spook fewer fish. That might be something. He gives at the knees to make himself smaller in the stream, and watches how, as water passes the rock, it leaves an eddy on each side. In that still water one could weigh anchor, let the stream bring food, look in on the current like a cafeteria window and make a choice. He sees into the water, to where the eddy sits, wedge-shaped, architectural. If you were invisible, would your rod be invisible too? And if the rod, then the fly line, and the fly?

He sees an invisible fly, under the surface, lodged in the lip of a fish. He doesn't see the fly disappear, he feels it—his arm has struck even before his mind's eye glimpses the take—and now he feels against his forearm the thick weight of a trout who has risen to sip in the hook. It is the handshake of an old friend. He looks to his arm amazed that it has done this thing without him, his hand now grasps the cork of the rod and he notices for the first time how his thumb, puckered against the rod butt, how down to its joint his thumb resembles nothing so much as a drumstick.

BACKHAND PUNCH CAST

PARGO

(FROM *MOONEY IN FLIGHT*)

Arden very much liked names. The words themselves don't matter, but it's a game, isn't it, knowing stuff like that? The first man who ate a pomegranate after calling it that still had seeds between his teeth. It doesn't build anything or move life anywhere, it's rather like the news. You can do without it, and most times it gets in the way, but it doesn't offend and it keeps you in touch with the human race, if you're so inclined.

The naming and the talk of tennis and the fishing got us easily through the days, and when my craving for a drink was about to send me off the deep end, a dose of anxiety over Arden neutralized it. She bunked downstairs, and I bunked up. The nights were tough. I wasn't used to sleep or sobriety. I paced the house and walked the beach and every so often I mounted the bulldozer intending to move it. Instead I'd sit and think about our day—get used to pleasure, Arden would tell me, it won't bite—think about our day and maybe peek in on her asleep, and I'd get through to the dawn.

Afternoons we would get out the fishing rod and stand to our knees together in the sizzling water to catch dinner. My casting was improving, but I couldn't match the lazy way she flipped the little pyramid sinker that pulled line out past the waves, plunking and settling. Or match her for knowing when to strike. Don't poke about, she would tell me. Sense it. Be that crab on the hook and you'll know when you're nibbled on. We caught little fish, jack and grunts, maybe a pound each. Dinner size. She knew their names, too, and she'd speak to them about the voyage on which their souls were embarking and their next appearance on earth, before she deftly bonked out their lights. Good eating, but little fish.

We talked. It was odd. When I spoke of my family, I saw not the people but cutouts where they had been. As a kid, Stace had these paper-doll books, you'd push out the doll and it left behind a gray cardboard outline. That's how I'd come to think of them.

Arden was interested in Tommy. Especially his paintings. Numinous worlds, she said when I described them, worlds of their own. We were standing in a warm surf and there was no action. I would have suggested quitting though it was pleasant there, the bubble and foam comforting, and Arden in her cotton sweatshirt with the sleeves pushed past her elbows like a teenager.

"You talk about him as if he's both a tragedy and a great success. You're half-right, he's a success."

"He is?" I wasn't about to take her word, though I wished I could, I wished she didn't have those studs in her nose.

"Yes. He has a lot of you in him. You are related etheric beings. He's out in the world and you're here, hiding behind booze and isolation. Inside you both lie the clarity and contentment you seek." She flung a cast beyond the swells and handed me the rod. I began a slow retrieve.

I meant to ask what Tommy had of me in him, but I didn't get the chance. Just as she finished her sentence, I felt a twang on the line. The pole angled over deeply, and the line on the reel sang out against the drag. "Hit him," she shouted, and I didn't know what she meant. "Hit him," she was pantomiming a jerk on the rod, so I jerked it. "Again, again," and I did.

The angle the line made into the water flattened when the fish ran from the blind tug, then increased as he dove. It was twilight, and in the red water the weight of the fish was deep and jagged. He flopped against the line, you could feel his head horsing and his body curling into a C-clamp. I looked over to Arden to see if she wanted to take the rod. Her eyes glistened. Her eyes fixed on the vee where the line went into the water. "That's a nice fish," she said to herself, pleased. When the fish ran to the deep, the reel couldn't keep up with the pull and I took three grudging steps farther into the ocean. With the rod butt stuck in my belly I cranked with my left hand and pumped the shaft with my right. The muscle in my forearm began to ache. She came around and put her fingers on the points of my hipbone.

"Don't let him pull me out to sea."

"No," she was watching closely. She held on lightly, as if she was a fighting chair and we had forgotten to buckle the strap. It didn't help but I liked it just the same.

"He'll tire himself. Let him. Don't fight when he's fighting. Let him fight the rod." I cranked and did as she said.

The line came to rest, snagged I thought, and heavy on the bottom. I pulled gently to dislodge it, but Arden said no, he's just resting, and he was. The line began to move again, outward. I would have tossed it all in if she hadn't been there. When the fish let me, I recovered line. Once, just beyond the waves, he surfaced. Burst a little plomp on the evening water, silver and pink, and dove again.

"Pargo," I heard in her breath behind me, and I thought maybe she was cursing the fish. I reeled in against the weight. Now he was closer, yards beyond the surf and her voice quieted with concern.

"You can't pull against the waves. If you do, you'll lose him. When the wash is going out, let him go."

The fish was tiring. I timed the swells. When they moved the seas to shore, I took in line. We brought him gingerly through the breaking surf. A last wave caught him and tossed him into us, the water to our knees. We walked the flopping thing, dead but for his gasp, back up the beach.

From the fight I'd thought he'd be the size of a dinghy, but he was only two feet long and, beached and put away, weighed maybe twenty pounds. Pink and fleshy, he had taken the hook between two dentines that could punch holes in a car door. Red snapper, Arden said, pargo. One of the great eating fishes and if I'd chance it, she would prepare it for me the way Michael did. I was going to say, Hang it by its heels, but I let it go. Michael was gone. And Arden had been after me to give up grudges. She said they weighed only on the people who carried them.

Arden slid one hand under the gills and lifted the fish between us. Then she shook my hand as if we might be taking a picture on a tourist pier. I wished we had, I wished we'd had a picture and I'd send it to the Clerk, and on the back I'd write, Dear Canges, Drop dead.

Arden cleaned the fish with Michael's knife and cut large steaks from its sides. I carried them to the house. She went down to the rocks. Mussels, she told me, for appetizers.

I wrapped the slabs of fish in newspaper and shelved them lengthwise in the refrigerator. When I went back to the beach, she had her clump of mussels and was stripping down to swim. I watched from the beach, she didn't seem to mind. There was not a line on her body. She swam way out, to where the lavender waters were smooth and groomed, like a golf course. Then she turned tail up and dove. The white buoy of her buttocks, then the points of her feet. Had she bottomed out? When she surfaced she swam parallel to the shore, around the point so I couldn't see her anymore, and finally, when I'd thought about God knows what, came swimming back. The way she stroked the water I wished it was me, the way each arm cocked at its own angle, an angle she made up, held over the black pudding-skin, and then slid magically in without a splash. She could make it to China.

IN THE BAG

LABOR DAY

She had come in for lunch every Friday since he'd worked there, which was too long. Always the same table, always the Stolyrocks-twist, always the face that she put on to accept the trophy as God's favorite angel. Usually she arrived with people from an office, responsible people who frowned when they spoke and talked on cell phones. Today she was alone.

"So. What are you doing for the long weekend?" He could not remember hearing her voice before.

"I don't know. Going fishing, I guess."

"Where?"

"I got this spot. Private water. The summer people will be gone." She had stone green eyes and a nervous finger that tapped Morse on the white cloth.

"Take me with you."

"You like to fish?"

"Never tried."

He served another sitting, a four-top that stayed until quarter of three. Then he found the assistant manager and quit.

• • •

He wasn't sure why he'd agreed. At first he thought she was bluffing, then that she wouldn't show, but when he drove up Saturday morning, she was standing in front of the restaurant. No gear, no satchel, no nothing. She expected to come home that night. That was OK. He would drive her back to the city and if the fishing was good, he could go back the next day. There was no rush. What he had most of was time.

She showed up in jeans and a bogus cowgirl shirt. The blouse looked like something from a TV square dance number, its snaps were mother-of-pearl. Her lipstick could have been chrome. Still, she was so beautiful it hurt his eyes.

"Where do you stay when you go fishing?"

"Me? I usually camp. I keep a bag in the trunk, a couple tarps."

"A bag."

"A sleeping bag."

"Oh," and she laughed.

"Why?" he said.

"Well, I wasn't sure. A body bag? a shopping bag? no, a handbag? Maybe a garbage bag? Maybe he sleeps in a garbage bag."

He was nervous and laughed too long.

"Well," and she lit a cigarette with a butane lighter the aqueous color of her eyes. "Well, I'm not camping."

"Never thought you were."

Once they got through the traffic it was an easy drive. He knew a creek that ran down the north face of the mountains, in a draw two exits beyond the ski area. Developers had recently found it, and now there were half a dozen mega-houses along the road, shake roofs, hot tubs, satellite dishes the size of a Dodge truck. But the stream fell down freestone from beaver ponds above and it held fish, you could always catch fish, and no one seemed to care it was there.

"So," she said impatiently as he made the turn up the valley. "You going to be a waiter all your life?"

"Not any more. Yesterday was my last day."

She rolled down the window and made to throw out the cigarette.

"Use the ashtray."

"There is no ashtray."

"Use the floor. That country's dry."

She considered his words, dropped the butt and rubbed it out under the toe of her lizard boot. "So what do you do?" he asked.

She waited a minute to answer. Or near enough.

"I manage money."

"I didn't know it needed managing."

She looked over to see whether he was serious but she couldn't tell.

"It does."

"You mean it's like hair? Or pets? If no one manages it, it gets unruly?"

"Something like that." Now he had her smiling.

"Like a Labrador puppy? It chews up shoes and shits on the floor?"

She laughed at that. Stuck her jaw into the air and laughed.

"I guess I've never had enough to know. None of my pocket change needs housebreaking."

When she laughed, her mouth stayed open after the sound ended. As if it had its own memory. He liked the way she did it.

"So what about you?" They were out of the car, and he was setting up two fly rods. Stringing them and tying on tippet.

"What about?"

"Now that you're not a waiter. What are you going to do?"

"I don't know. Work up here for the winter."

She looked around. Prospects didn't appear to her.

"Doing what?"

"I'll get on at the ski area. Drive a Cat. Run a lift. Something like that." He knotted a pale morning dun onto one rod and onto the other a little pheasant tail nymph he had tied that morning. He knew this water. What you used wasn't as important as how you used it.

"The snow melts, though. Doesn't that usually happen? Doesn't the snow melt in spring?"

"Usually does."

"So? Back to waiting tables?"

He shrugged. "That's April. This is September."

"Got to have a plan."

"Do I?" He pulled the line through and flicked a gentle false cast to take out the twists. "I don't know. Maybe Idaho. I got a friend would put me on."

"Doing what?"

"Running boats. Middle Fork of the Salmon."

"What's that?"

This time it was he who looked over suspiciously. "It's a river."

"Oh," she said. "I thought maybe it was part of a place setting."

She didn't care about fishing. He showed her how to handle a fly rod, how to get the cast out and watch so that it coiled back and straightened. "It should look like a cat's tail," he said as the line looped out in a curl. "It should just lay out on the back cast and then," his forearm moving easily, "do the same thing forward."

"A cat's tail," she repeated. "I like that."

He put her hand on top of his, so she would get the feel of the rod's loading, of the tension, the release. Under the shirt, the rodeo-queen shirt, the muscles of her shoulder worked smoothly. Shouldn't wear cotton on the stream, he thought to say. Stays wet all day. But he said nothing.

"Now you try it." He arranged her hand in the proper grip. Put his own on hers gently.

"Switching positions, huh?" she said with a smile, but he ignored her.

126

She walked behind him. When he fished she stood to the left and chatted. He took a couple of brookies from the stream. Little fish that he eased off the hook once he'd shown her their magical coloring. They passed a last house that had been locked up for the season, a sprawling place with gates and No Trespassing signs.

"Some joint, huh?" he asked. "Imagine having a house like this and not using it?"

"They use it," she said as if she knew the owners. "A month in the summer. Christmas week and then, when the kids are off, spring vacation."

"Seems a pity," he said.

She was unsympathetic. "When they divorce he'll take the one in town. The salable one. Fob this one off on her."

Upstream from the house lay a line of ponds. The land flattened into a small park. Young aspen surrounded the stream, and their tender bark had lured in beavers. This was the place for stealth, he told her. His eyes watched the water. "The fly doesn't matter here, they'll hit anything. But you can't let them hear you or see you. They're spooky."

"Why?" she whispered back.

"Look at the water. Shallow. Clear. They're easy pickings for hawk, owls."

Throughout the acre-pond, she saw shadows cruising easily, feeding occasionally on the surface. It looked like the workings of a watch.

"Tough life," she whispered.

She had been carrying the rod with the nymph. He took it from her and greased its line. Then he let out a false cast over the bank, so its shadow wouldn't fall on the water. When he rolled the line out over the pond, it fell to the surface without a ripple. Still, two fish scampered for cover. He began a slow and twitching retrieve. The nymph lay on the surface. In the bright sun they could see it clearly, though it was the size of a fingernail cutting. Clearly in the clear water, for it was borne on a tiny bead of water of its own gravity. The fur of its body gathered water to it, changed the refraction of light, caught the trout's attention.

Carefully, he made the nymph move across the surface, across a submerged aspen trunk that rested in soft decay on the bottom. From under the trunk a trout larger than the rest rose to see what this was. In one breath the fish inhaled it and began to sink back.

He struck. Softly so as not to spook the hooked trout. The line went taut. There were too many obstacles to play this fish. He reeled it in quickly, his fingers snagged its open jaw and he removed the hook. It was a cutthroat, its belly Moroccan yellow against the black-green lens of the water.

"Why'd you let him go?" she asked. "He was big enough. He would have made dinner."

"We'll stop to eat on the way back," he said. "I'll buy you a steak. Nothing pretty about a steak."

They walked back, he again in the lead. She spoke as they arrived at the house at the head of the trail. "I don't want to go back. Let's stay the night."

He looked. The blinds were drawn to keep out the high country sun.

She insisted. "They're not here. We'll borrow their place."

She took his hand and went up to the front door. It was locked. Just in case she put her shoulder to it. She had him lift her by the waist so she could inspect the shelf above the doorjamb, and again in the back.

"It's not our house," he said but in his voice he heard the rasp of desire.

"Shit," she said. "That's where we keep ours."

They walked the perimeter of the fence, both feeling under the rough underside of the cross timber. He wasn't sure what he wanted. Trespassing on land was one thing, breaking and entering another. What he wanted, he realized, didn't matter. That fish didn't want to get caught.

Finally, around the back, they found it. She lifted the lid of the cedar bin for the garbage cans, heavy and latched to discourage bear and raccoon, and let out a whoop.

"See," she said proudly. She held up the spare key, dangling from a loop of braided blue and white lanyard.

Inside she was at ease. The house had handsome leather furniture and Navajo rugs. She found the bar and poured herself a vodka with ice. "It needs something. Peppercorns," she said, and went off to the kitchen. He followed. "Some people prefer lemon peel or onion, but some days peppercorn adds just the right bitterness."

She walked him through the house as if it were hers. From address labels on magazines she determined that the owners lived in Chicago. "Maybe not," he said. "After all, these magazines are all about houses. Maybe this house subscribes, maybe it wants to read about friends who are houses." On the walls were antique ski posters and shelves of kachina dolls. There was a log-railed balcony, of which she approved, and a settee covered in zebra hide, of which she did not. She knew a great deal about the rugs. She showed him the Storm Pattern and the Klagetoh, the Ganado Red and the Burnt Water.

"You're really into this. Weaving."

"They're collectibles, silly." She poured a second vodka. "Native American. Hot market. The average rug, say three by five, has about eight warp and twenty-five weft threads per inch. That requires over 300 hours of work." He decided to take a beer from the refrigerator. One bedroom housed a massive bed with down quilts. Beyond its dressing suite there were his-and-her bathrooms that adjoined a large, stone-floor shower. He folded the quilts into ungainly squares, and they made love on the bed.

"We can stay the night," she said. "There's spaghetti and sauce in the cupboards and for breakfast, cereal. We'll have to use dry milk."

She wanted a fire but he refused. The place was so clean, he didn't want to leave soot over their furniture. Besides, he'd have to get on the roof to make sure they had a spark guard. Instead, after dinner, they undressed and ran the hot tub. Stars came out and chilled the air. When the timer shut off they lay on the deck and watched the water evaporate from their skin into the thin night. She mixed herself a large vodka, without the peppercorns.

They made love again. This time he fetched one of the quilts and wrapped it about them.

"Isn't that a wedding ring?" he asked.

She looked at her finger as if someone had recently stuck it on her hand—grow this for me, I'll be back for it.

"No. No, actually that's a guard ring. Notice how the baguettes are set to reflect light back into the main stone." She removed it with a twist.

"And that is an engagement ring." She removed that too. "This last, *that's* a wedding ring." She jangled the three in her hand and then, in a weak, left-handed throw, cast them against the far wall.

He slept lightly. By resolve, so he could hear any car approach. He figured how he would gather their things, lead her out through the deck. The spaghetti and vodka and Pepperidge Farm macadamia cookies he'd have to replace by mail. Still, he must have been dozing when she came at him.

She pushed his shoulder a second time, and he woke preparing to flee.

"Love me," she said.

"Listen. I'm tired."

"Love me," she said again and bit down hard on his shoulder. He yelled, and she struck at his face. She had no strength and from where she lay no purchase, so the blow glanced off his turned head.

"Hey," he said and grabbed her wrists. She was flailing now. "Love me, God damn it." She wailed and shouted at him. Some words he couldn't make out, and he wasn't certain she was awake. He was frightened so he kept her pinned to the bed. Finally, when she began to cry, he relented his grip and put his arms loosely about her. She cried and moaned. He held her that way until she fell back asleep.

In the morning he made a pitcher of orange juice from a can in the freezer, fresh coffee, and two bowls of Rice Krispies. The powdered milk did up fine. He retrieved her rings and put them on her night table as if she'd taken them off before retiring. She hardly ate. He did up the dishes, laundered the sheet, and replaced the cover on the hot tub. They were on the road by nine.

"So," he felt the need to say something. "What will you do for Labor Day? That's tomorrow."

"Wear white."

"What do you mean?"

"You can't wear white after Labor Day. Tomorrow's my last chance. So I think I'll wear white."

He was heartened to see she had put on all three rings.

He dropped her at the restaurant. It was closed for the holiday, but he assumed she had parked her car nearby.

"Listen," he said through the open window. "Are you going to be OK?"

Her eyes widened with an amused, mad twinkle. For a moment he feared she was going to get hysterical again.

"No. Of course not."

He pulled away slowly. In his mind he was compiling a shopping list. He could sneak back in and restock. The vodka for sure, although he wasn't sure he could duplicate the Polish brand they had. The spaghetti and a jar of the sauce, the cookies. He didn't think they would miss the cereal or the dry milk.

PALS

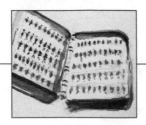

THE RETREAT
(FROM *MARITAL ASSETS*)

I packed a small grip, called the office to tell them I might not be in next week, and drove to the family house in Litchfield County. It sits on a lake, and most of the houses are summer places, though, with the interest in Nordic skiing, there are often people at the homes and at the one or two resorts on the lake all winter. The unseasonably mild spell had melted the snow, and now, as I drove up the gravel drive, I realized that there was no one around. The solitude and quiet of the house made me think I had made a mistake, and I contemplated driving in to Danbury and staying at a motel. Instead, I built a fire in the parlor, poured myself a large Scotch and soda, and went around switching on lights and turning up thermostats.

By the time I had made my rounds and a second drink I was feeling much better. Ages ago, I had put in a store of tinned goods in the pantry behind the kitchen for just such an unplanned visit, and I rummaged through the cans of stew, soups, sardines and hash planning a meal. I opened a tin of smoked oysters and ate them with soda crackers and a third drink, while a pot of vegetable soup came to a boil on the stove.

Only a trained monk can contemplate in the time he sets aside for it. To the rest of us, thought comes like hail in the summer and insight like snow. I found myself regretting my decision to throw out the television set in the country house, as I sat spinning the radio dial in an unsuccessful search for music without amplified guitars. Hey, said one disc jockey to me, if it's too loud, you're too old.

I ate the soup as the fire burned down. Perhaps I would read through the evening. I took down a volume of Sherlock Holmes from the shelves, but I was unable to concentrate through a paragraph, even on stories I knew well. Three drinks are beyond my capacity.

I walked out on the porch and listened. There was nothing, no sound. Too late in the day for road noises, too early in the year for crickets. I heard a wooden squeak and realized it was the ancient board of the porch under my own weight. The silence had a vitality, its own single breath, not in or out but a single breath without break. I spoke my own name and listened. Far off a car's engine murmured and died away. I could see my breath condensing in the air, but it made no sound. Across the lake I saw the light of another house. I stared at it, and as if preternaturally I heard the thin voice of something from inside of it. The siren of an ambulance from a television set or the cry of a child or a violin's cadenza. I couldn't tell, and it didn't matter. Satisfied, the silence broken, I went inside.

• • •

I came away with no insights from that weekend, and few enough recollections. For some reason I remember getting into bed that first night. I chose to sleep in a single bed in the room that had been mine as a child. When it had been last made I don't know, but its flannel sheets were fresh and cool. Like a glass of water left standing. On its top rested a quilt of precise pattern, forest green diamonds hosting bunches of yellow, orange, and purple asters. The quilt had been in the house for ages. I pulled it back and, folding it into quarters, placed it carefully on a chair in the corner.

At the head were two pillows. The one underneath was oversized, with a coarse filling. The other was of fine down fitted into a percale case. The bed had been made with almost military tautness, and the top sheet was pulled over the grey wool blanket a satisfying six inches. Like a man's cuff showing just the right amount of linen. The bed struck me as a prospect of great stability. To come in the dark upon this perfectly made bed, cool sheets on a frosting February night with the promise of one's own body heat to warm the space, to spend the time suspended with one's own thoughts, cozy, alone.

For the rest of the weekend I occupied my time. We had had a cord of wood delivered that needed splitting, and I took the ash-handled axe to that task. I've always enjoyed chopping wood. The trick is to chop through it, to hit for the stump and not the log. It took hours and I ached from the exercise, but by sundown on Saturday I had separate piles of pine, apple, and oak, all but the apple—too small in diameter to split—quartered and stacked on the side porch.

On Sunday morning I went into town for breakfast, and read the *New York Times* over a meal I assumed Paul Bunyan would have cooked for himself. The day was clear, the light was bright and blue enough to make a sound. Afterwards, towards noon, I walked from our house to the marshy creek that feeds into the north end of the lake. There at the water's edge I could see the inaudible commotion of a hatch of insects. The warmth of the past weeks had brought them out prematurely. It was a hundred mayflies, hatching off the surface. The order Ephemeroptera, ephemeral, short-lived. I knew about them from my sketching. The summer I was twelve I collected water insects and drew them. Mayflies had been my favorites, delicate forms with gauzy wings, each a perfectly rounded deltoid, a satisfying shape to draw.

A little cloud of them carried off downstream. Light shone through the bare trees, the maple and birch, dappling the ground with shadow. Pattern over pattern. The husk of some seed blew in the breeze, lifting off to follow the path of the mayflies now out of view.

SUMMERTIME

TYING THE
WHIP FINISH

W hat if she had received without histrionics his announcement
that he was letting an apartment, a statement she viewed as
proof that he would not be back, that he would be free to conduct his
affair—which he fervently and regularly denied—out from under the
canopy of guilt and complication, proof that this separation was not
temporary as he pretended but the final and inevitable retreat of a
coward, indeed a statement the interpretation of which, unlike so
much else in their lives, they shared?

When the announcement was over, he descended the narrow wood
stairs to the basement. He kept his tying bench in the corner that had
served as a coal bin. Slatted walls framed in the cubicle, tongue-in-
groove boards painted cream, an odd choice for their function. They
were chipped to the grain from years of bombardment. The single window, high up to accommodate the chute, was nailed shut. He had a
recurring thought about the space, and he had it now: curious, coal
stored in cellars, a pile of heat you laid down in the fall and depleted
night by night, a clumsy gauge of time and comfort.

He had made the corner homey, with a square of carpet, a CD player, a lamp to supplement the bare bulb. Now he considered what music to play, running a finger across the squared plastic cases. Opera was his choice when he tied. And particularly this one, this was a favorite.

He turned on the gooseneck lamp—he should attend to it, the switch wiggled in its fitting—and swung the glass out of the way. He would not need magnification to tie streamers. Muddler minnows for the slack days of summer. It was a tactic that lacked the precision of dry-fly fishing. Bounce the muddler off the bank, let it sink, and then bring it in with a twitched retrieve.

They had always taken a summer float together. She was remarkably adept. She cast adequately, but she had a feel for the sport and an uncanny knack of spotting fish. Not he. He fished blind. He told himself his edge was intuition, but the truth, when he had to face it, was he simply didn't see the fish as well as she. She always out-fished him. When they floated, she took the bow until she tired of standing, but when she was catching fish, she could last the day.

The opera is set in the time of the French Revolution. A young poet invited to an elegant ball is asked to compose an ode. He extemporizes, and his poem speaks of the terrible inequities between rich and poor. His honesty and insight win the heart of the beautiful Madeleine.

He lined up his materials in the order he would use them. Set out a dozen hooks and crimped their barbs. You didn't want to put the energy into dressing a fly only to find later, flattening down the barb, you snapped it off. He placed a spool of lead wire by the hooks. Then the turkey feather, chenille for the body, the fine gauge gold wire he would use as a rib, and a patch of deer hair. Finally the hackle. No need for expensive hackle—these flies were supposed to sink—and good dry-fly hackle would be a waste. He bent a russet saddle so the

points of its feathers stood against the light, and examined their bar-
bules. Some web, but supple. Perfect for a streamer.

The Revolution has taken hold, and the poet is in danger because
of his associations with the aristocracy. Tumbrels with the day's condemned roll by as he sits at a café. His friends implore him to flee, but
he has fallen in love.

If she had not reacted so emotionally, they might have talked
themselves through it. It wasn't as if the announcement came as news
to either one. He knew it was coming, and he knew she knew as well.
So why the ranting and grieving? Why the unkind words? Couldn't
she simply allow them both some civility?

That was not her way. If she spotted a fish, she cast to it. If she
caught it, she killed it. She moved through life with purpose filed to a
sharp point.

He wrapped the thread carefully. Each coil lay ribbed next to the
last, no break in the winding. Then tied on a tag of turkey feather for
the tail and lay down a base of lead wire. With each fly he would take
one more turn of the lead, so that when the flies were set in the box,
they presented a spectrum of weights, light to heavy, depending on
how deep he wanted to go. Success is all in the preparation.

The poet has been betrayed by his friends and is imprisoned. To
save him, Madeleine goes to his rival, now a member of the council
that holds the power of life and death. She offers herself for her lover's
freedom. The rival is moved by her beauty and by her sentiment.

He completed the body, ribbed it with gold tinsel, tied in the
curled wing and the hackle, and added the deer hair for the head. He
repeated the process eleven times. All the while, *André Chénier* played
on the machine. Not until he had finished the dozen, identical to the
eye but each peculiar in its density, not until then would he take up
the last tasks. It was more efficient to do the final trimming, tying the
whip finish and lacquering the knot, as discrete tasks. To trim the deer

hair, he would use the magnifying glass, and doing them together avoided refocusing his eyes. Constant adjustments in focus gave him a headache. And the lacquering—the cement was particularly volatile. If the jar were left open, the cement dried out.

He arranged the tools he would need. Brought the glass in front of the tying vice, laid out the scissors, opened the jar. The fumes gave him a quick high—given half a chance, he could become a glue sniffer. He smiled at the prospect. His friends would not suspect him, meticulous in all his habits, of substance abuse. That was not his nature. He trimmed the hair on each of the twelve flies into a precise bullet.

The poet is in prison, writing a love song. Madeleine arrives. She has bribed the guards to let her take the place of another woman, a woman condemned to die the next day. She desires to perish with her lover. Her wish is gratified, and as dawn breaks, they ascend the scaffold together.

It was while he was tying the whip finish that she left the house. He sensed it. The closing door made a noise, certainly, but the music was swelling to a crescendo and he didn't actually hear anything. What told him of her exit was a compression of air in the house. She would be walking to the garage. He wasn't sure how he knew, but he knew it. Like casting to the fish. He knew that was where she was headed.

The whip knot is tied with a small tool that wraps the thread about the shaft of the hook and pulls the end through. He enjoyed the whip finish—he was dexterous and could shape the knot by decreasing the number of wraps as the knot wound towards the eye of the hook. He watched through the glass as the thread formed a perfect taper.

He still had time. She took a while to settle in, keys, glasses, garage-door opener. He could intercept the car as it backed down the drive. They could talk.

But the cement was opened. It evaporated so quickly. By the time he got back, it would have congealed. He touched the tiny brush into the liquid and, squinting through the magnifying glass, daubed its tip to the black cone that was the knot.

BLOOD KNOT MASTER

THE PIOUS
ANGLER

When one of our foursome canceled it didn't occur to me that the outfitter would stick in a sub. You don't expect a replacement for an ill bridegroom, and the ritual that is our annual fishing trip is no less sacramental.

I can't remember how it started. The four of us used to hang out as kids, and ages ago we decided to begin again. We've grown too old to camp, so we skip the food tasting of ash and the sleeping bags, and instead pick a spot with proper beds, good cuisine, and ample whiskey. Kevin abandons his trading desk deep in the Manhattan bowels—does Manhattan have any other body parts? Jake declares a week's vacation; at close of summer break I'm often researching some minor event in Colonial history, so I give up the least. Ed's our fourth. We meet in the west—Kevin is flush, he can afford the travel, and the rest of us are here—and we find a Rocky Mountain river that has been coursing through our dreams.

This year it was wonderful tail water in southeastern Idaho, trickling off the backside of the Tetons. It was Ed who went on the Net and found a farmhouse that two guides had converted into a B&B. Two guides, four fisherman, three days of superior fishing during the brown drake hatch. And it was Ed who cancelled.

Kevin and Jake flew into Jackson Hole, I drove out to meet their planes, and we raced our rental car over Fox Creek Pass into Idaho.

• • •

It was just what you would hope—a simple farmhouse set in a long, easy hayfield that had turned golden in the summer heat. Inside no antimacassars or ruby glass swans, just sensible stuff—four bedrooms, breakfast and dinner in the expanded kitchen, everything geared to the fishermen. A gray, pudgy woman ran the place. Mrs. Henders had a goiter the size of grapefruit and a fussy way, but she scurried out as soon as she'd shown us around upstairs. Shown us our rooms and remarked to the closed door on the second floor,

"That'll be the fourth gentleman."

"Fourth? There's no fourth."

"Oh yes. The boys reserve the right to fill the boats, you know. We got a single just this past week."

We looked at each other. Ed wasn't one for fine print.

"He's very quiet." This to explain him. "From the East, like one of you." Here she looked about and, not wanting to be mistaken, we pointed to Kevin. "He'll be no bother. Eats in his room."

"In his room?"

"Brought his own food. Quiet and I have to say a little . . . strange. Well," she said turning her back to us. "Dinner at eight. Breakfast at seven. The boys will be here to pick you up."

The news tripped me up. The prospect of an interloper in our midst was disheartening. This was our week to act silly, share that nostalgia for adolescence male friends seem never to abandon. It comes from swallowing our secrets and failings, and the nostalgia passes for intimacy. An extra presence promised a different mix. A lot depended on who the fourth fisherman was.

We didn't find out at dinner. True to our housekeeper's word, the mystery man stayed in his room. "He brought his own food," she told us again in a whisper, her eyes darting up the staircase as if reading for Jane Eyre.

Whatever disappointment we suffered Mrs. Henders erased with a call to the kitchen.

"This is Sherree. She waits tables."

"The farmer's daughter," said Jake breathlessly.

"No, mine," Mrs. Henders answered, an unclipped barb in her voice.

An angel's face, oval and flawless, except for maybe the Gene Tierney overbite. Chestnut hair in a 'Forties pageboy, eyes that were Big-Sky blue, a healthy size twelve crammed enthusiastically into a size ten blouse and jeans. The effort revealed certain attributes that often appeal to superficial males.

"Sherry," Jake said in his game-show host voice. "After the fortified wine from Spain."

"No, two Es."

"Two Es," Jake repeated, captivated. "And two lovely E's if I may say so." No one knew what he meant, but he and Sherree giggled. "Two Es at the end?"

"Yes." This all discussed with the seriousness that attended the choice of dry fly.

"Then three Es if you count the one in the middle. You mustn't forget the one in the middle."

I don't know how growing up in Eastern Idaho affects a pretty twenty-something girl's perception of sophistication and banter. Sherree reacted to these commonplaces as if Jake were the soul of wit, with a delighted squeal.

Jake is something of a swordsman. He cannot meet a woman between six and sixty and not try to forge a secret bond. It doesn't lead
anywhere, or at least not when he's in the open, and it is always appre-
ciated. This little tic hasn't interfered with his marriage—his wife
either doesn't know or doesn't care. In restaurants, in lines at airports
and rental car counters, every year we watch his antics, and later listen
to him spin fantasies as we float the rivers.

It's embarrassing, but we're all peculiar. Kevin is obsessed with
electronics and I worry over George Washington's military tactics.

"Look at that," Jake breathed as Sherree retreated to the kitchen
with the news of how we liked our steaks. "This is going to be a great
trip. Rising trout, the Wild West, and dinners served by the ambassa-
dor from the Central Hooterville Republic."

We poured ourselves a second round of martinis from the shaker
Jake always brings, and uncorked a red wine he wanted us to fuss over.
The owners of the place, the website made clear, were LDS—Latter
Day Saints, Mormons. They didn't serve alcohol, but they had no
objection to guests bringing their own, so long as it was used in moder-
ation. Mrs. Henders' cooking was up to the claret Kevin had supplied.

After dinner we went into the parlor. Randy and Cort—the
guides—had set up a vice for the guests' use and I sat down to tie
ginger quills for the next day's outing. Jake went back and forth to
the kitchen. The way an antsy retriever on the hunt wants to hurry
you along. He was sitting with us, reporting on his progress, when the
stairs creaked and the fourth fisherman appeared.

Strike me dead. He was a tall man who walked with a stoop. At
first you couldn't tell whether he was old or young, white or black,
because of his outfit. He wore a white shirt with no tie, a vest buttoned at every chance, and a black jacket down to his knees. Dr. Jekyll
would have called it a frock coat. Below the vest hung dirty-looking
tassels, like hair that needed a wash. His own hair, long and ropey, hung

out from under the gloom of his hat so you couldn't tell what was hair and what was shadow.

And the hat—mostly he was hat, a man hanging down from a hat. You've seen those jellyfish that are all tentacles, wisps from a giant umbrella. His hat was the umbrella. It was black, more pelt than metallic, with a round, unshaped crown that was overly tall. The brim reached to his shoulders and swallowed the light under it. To find his face you had to stare, you couldn't be sure it hadn't disappeared.

We didn't know what to say. Our eyes were on the hat. Finally Jake came up with something to break the silence.

"I see by your outfit that you are a cowboy."

He smiled. I know because yellow teeth glinted out from the midst of the cloud.

"How do you do?" He spoke with great formality and wiped the palm of a hand on his lapel. "I believe we are fishing together. I sincerely thank you for welcoming me into your circle."

He stuck the hand into space, a bluish-white thing that seemed to be attached to nothing, so I rose and took it. I gave him my name.

"And mine is Chaim Leibovits. I am glad to make your acquaintance."

I shook the frail thing, hoping it wouldn't break off. Jake and Kevin followed suit.

"Hayim," said Jake.

"Chaim," said Chaim, clearing his throat to make the sound.

"Kayim," said Kevin.

"Chaim," said Chaim. "It means life."

"Oh," Kevin said and pointed as if he recognized him. "'To life, to life, l'Kayim.'"

"Precisely." Chaim seemed pleased.

"You know the song? From the movie?"

Chaim pursed his lips. "I don't go to movies."

"Or the play?" Jake asked. "It was on Broadway."

"I don't go to plays."

We were stalemated. Sherree broke it, stepping in to announce her departure. Jake grabbed a jacket and left to walk her home. It turned out she and her mother lived down the block.

"We may never see him again," mused Kevin.

"But he is a married man," said Chaim. "He wears a ring."

"Kevin was making a joke," I explained, though I didn't believe it.

Chaim nodded. He made an awkward bow and excused himself. "I have studying. They will come for us at seven?"

"Or seven-thirty."

Chaim bowed again and withdrew.

"He doesn't go to movies," Kevin said to me. "He doesn't get jokes. We're in for a long weekend."

I shrugged and went back to the vice. Ginger quills were the fly for mid-September. I wanted a dozen for the next day.

"What are we going to do?"

"We're here for three days. Each of us gets Chaim," I did the gargle thing better than the others, "one day. Unless you want to volunteer?"

"You suppose he fishes in those clothes?"

"I'd bet yes."

"Maybe it's better than khaki. Maybe the fish think he's come to bless them."

I gave Kevin four ginger quills. "We'll see soon enough."

• • •

At breakfast, Jake gave us no clues about the Battle of Sherree Bluffs. He delighted in sharing what defenses had been raised to the initial landing, but so long as the outcome of the invasion was unsure, like any good officer he kept his tactics close to his vest.

The meal was excessive: Colorado cantaloupe, thick-cut bacon, and blueberry pancakes, made with berries from a neighbor's bushes.

We were in the midst of it when Cort and Randy arrived. We introduced ourselves around. Cort called up the stairwell and Chaim soon descended.

"Hayim," Jake announced, "you and I will fish together, if that's OK." For all his appetites, Jake is a kind man who loves to teach people his sport. He assumed, as we all did, that this exotic Jew—I'd explained to my mates that he was a Hasid, though they had no idea what was meant by the word—was a newcomer to the world of casting, bugs, and the strategies of fly fishing.

Kevin and I set off with our guide. Our McKenzie boat was in the water by nine. The Teton River was running fast and clear, and the fishing was so lively that Kevin didn't pull out his cell to check the markets until well into the morning.

"Give it a rest," I said from the stern when he'd come back to us. "What do you mean?"

"The phone. Leave it home. You're on vacation."

He waved me off. "What do you know? You teach history."

"Does that disqualify me from recognizing anti-social behavior?" Just about this time my indicator fly, a large Goddard caddis you couldn't miss, disappeared on a tangent. I struck. It was the sixteen-inch rainbow and not my argument that brought Kevin back. He tied on a nymph and began a furious series of casts to catch up.

"No," he came back to the conversation once his line was in the water. "But you don't understand. In my business I have to stay close. Solly called my desk looking for $100 million in the note. We don't respond they go somewhere else. This is Solly, understand."

"Tell Solly to come out here and bring a rod." Solly is Salomon Brothers, that much I know. Kevin trades treasury bills. When institutions are moving out of the market, the money all goes into T-bills. If one institution is a seller, often they all are. Kevin's job is to quote the highest price possible and not lose the sale, except if the next buyer would pay more. It moves more quickly than U. S. history.

"You don't tell Solly, they tell you. Hey, that gives me an idea . . ."

He stowed his line and got the cell back out. I landed my rainbow, caught a second before he put his phone away.

We renewed the conversation over lunch. Kevin couldn't see my point, nor I suppose I his. It was a vacation; he was supposed to get away. He insisted you couldn't just walk off when people depended on you. I said he was refusing to recognize that the hitch in his cast developed because, indeed, they didn't depend on you.

In any event, until the closing bell rang, as Kevin put it, we had uninterrupted fishing. Except for one call to the man covering for him and a text message or two to see where the thirty-year bond closed. On the whole it was a good day. Floating through that canyon would refresh the soul of a stone.

Back at our rooms, we showered and changed for cocktails. We were at least two up on the other pair when they walked in.

Chaim gave a jerky bow, mostly in the neck, the way a pigeon moves.

"How did you do?" Kevin asked.

"A wonderful day," Chaim said. He was still in the suit, still under the hat. "Everything I expected and more. I will see you gentlemen tomorrow." He bowed again and we wished him goodnight. I had the sinking feeling that something was wrong. Jake headed upstairs to shower. Kevin and I looked at each other ominously, but we would have to wait for the story.

Cleaned and dressed, Jake poured himself a bourbon and water to bring to dinner. When Sherree entered with the soup, he said hello. Warm and courteous, but not the one we expect, the hello that means I can see through your clothes.

Jake has revealed to us several tricks of his trade. A never-miss, he insists, is to compliment a woman on her shoes. So Kevin gave him a little needle.

"Those are wonderful sneakers, Sherree. Where did you find them?"

As she told us of the wonders of the Pocatello WalMart, Kevin caught his eye. But Jake seemed unconcerned.

"So?" Kevin said when it was just the three of us again.

"So?" Jake came back.

"So tell us. How was your day with the rabbi?"

"He's not a rabbi," Jake said seriously. "A rabbi is a teacher, and he's a student. As I get it, he will be all his life. But I'll tell you this, he outfished me."

"He outfished you? Did you see his gear? It was cheap thirty years ago when it came from Montgomery Ward."

"What did you talk about?" I asked.

"The usual stuff. Flies, patterns, feeding. The guide and I both listened. Hayim knows his stuff."

Whatever had happened, Jake was a changed man. Sherree came in with dessert, a delicious tangle of yellow cake, Palisades peaches and ice cream. She hung around—her story was she was making sure we liked it.

She cleared the dishes, and came clean.

"Are you going to walk me home, Jake?"

"No, sweetheart. I just wanted to make sure the way was safe. I think tonight you can do it on your own."

A changed man. We coaxed him to tell us what happened, but Jake was having none of it.

We took our coffee into the living room. The furniture was comfortable, arts and crafts, lots of books on fly fishing, Idaho history, and the Emigration of the Saints. Kevin made up a shaker of stingers, a tradition, and we sat around sipping.

"So," Kevin said, still probing. "You enjoyed your day?"

"Very much," Jake said. "I think you will too. And if you two want to float together, I'd be happy to fish with him both days."

Kevin excused himself to go outside with his cell. Not manners, reception. I sensed an opportunity. I jerked my head toward the darkened kitchen. "You've recalled the troops?"

"She's a nice girl," Jake said, meaning, I'm sure, something different from what our grandparents did by the phrase.

"So what happened?"

Jake eluded the question. "Wonderful day. I got some on dries towards evening. Your ginger quill worked. But for numbers, I couldn't keep up with Hayim."

"I didn't mean with fish. I meant with you."

He studied his coffee cup.

"We did a lot of talking."

"So, you were converted?"

"Nothing like that. He's not preachy. Mostly he tells stories."

"Stories." I couldn't imagine what had gone on. "Like what?"

Jake weighed my confidence. We've been close over the years, talk about everything together. Except anything important.

"I'll tell you one. He said he'd noticed me. With Sherree. Said I reminded him of someone."

"Who?"

"There was a man in this town. Some name with lots of Ch in it." He made the gargling sound. "A man who loved women."

"Just like you." He ignored me.

"All kinds. But he was married. To what Hayim called a woman of valor. He knew he was doing wrong. Just playing at it, you understand. Although from the story you couldn't tell whether or not the guy was scoring."

"Just like you." Jake gave a tight smile.

"So anyway, on this holy day, you're supposed to take account of yourself, mend your ways. So he goes to see the rabbi.

"He tells the rabbi how he's addicted to women and how he can't help himself. The rabbi knows him, knows his family—this is some small town in Poland, unpronounceable—and he says to the man, Tonight I want you to go home, take off your belt and use it to beat your beautiful children.

"Well, the guy is shocked. He goes home, has dinner, and comes back to see the rabbi. 'I can't do it. Give me something else.'

"The rabbi shrugs. 'OK. Tonight, after supper let the fire burn. Stick the poker in the embers. At bed time, take it out and lay it across the flesh of your wife's back.'

"The guy is beginning to think the rabbi's nuts. I asked, why didn't he just get a new rabbi, and Kayim said, you don't do that.

"So the guy ignores him a second day. He comes back intending to tell the rabbi no more advice.

"The rabbi beats him to the draw. 'It's odd,' he says. 'You won't whip your children but you'll risk the abandonment and shame they'll suffer by you chasing your dick. You won't lay a hot poker on your wife's flesh but you'll scar her heart forever. I can give you no more advice. I must return to my studies, to learn where in the teachings of our ancestors you can possibly find a distinction.'"

Jake looked up. "That was it."

"And that's convinced you?"

"There were lots of stories. And sayings. He asked if we were married in a church, and when I said yes, he told me, 'When a man and wife divorce, even the altar weeps.'"

Kevin returned, ending our conversation with the problematic news that The Fed was dealing with higher inflation readings and slowing growth indicators. He is frantic to succeed, to move up the scale. In the castes of government trader, Kevin has explained to me, no one is lower than the bill trader. He deals in tiny margins, a basis point is a hundredth of a percent, and makes less than anyone else on the trading floor, which, as I get it, is between ten and a thousand times what I make.

• • •

Friday morning we decided Jake and I would fish together. Sabbath began at sundown, Chaim needed to prepare. Kevin was happy to cut the day short, so he could call in his weekend trading strategy.

We had a slow day. The sun was summer hot and in the clear water, tippet lay on the surface like barge cable. Toward the end, under the shade of the first wisps of cirrus, the fish began to move, but on the whole it was a frustrating day.

I expected Kevin to be furious. He comes the farthest, he picks the time of year. He also has this Big City view that each of his minutes should show a profit—if he's fishing, the fish need to take notice. It comes from living among raging ambitions, where serenity can't buy itself a congregation or a cathedral. We sat on the porch of the rooming house, consoling ourselves with tall tonic drinks, the three of us, telling our tales of woe.

Darkness settled. The screen door opened and Chaim appeared. He still wore that preposterous hat, but under it he had dressed in a white velvet suit. He looked like a comic book hero, from an 18th century comic book.

"Hayim," Jake called. "Tell us you're not throwing it all in for a career in Vegas."

He gave his pigeon dip, and though his face was bathed in shadow, I think a ripple of appreciation crossed his face. "I simply wanted to wish you," he spoke formally, "my fishing compatriots, a good Shabbos. And to thank you for allowing me to join your party."

We returned the wishes. He addressed me.

"Our Shabbos lasts until sunset tomorrow. But I have a special dispensation allowing me to fish. I will meet you at the river."

I told him Cort intended to put in ten miles upstream. We'd all drive up together.

"My dispensation is to do the fly fishing, not to break a Commandment. Our laws prohibit riding on the Sabbath."

"Cut yourself some slack, Hayim," Jake said. With Sherree out of the picture he had charm to spare. "Who will know?"

"Who indeed?" Chaim said. He then jerked his thumb skyward and gave—hard to be sure in the fading light with that dark cloud on his head—a wink.

"So you'll walk to the put-in?"

"I'll walk. I'll study. I'll think. When you arrive, I'll fish."

Ten miles. Both of my pals groaned.

"Please excuse us," I told him. "We just want you to have the comforts we have. You're stuck with nonbelievers."

"I understand. You want us all to be alike. It is only human." And without a beat he launched a story.

"The Tsar comes to the great Tanhum and says, 'Rabbi, your people and mine would stop being enemies if we became one people.'

"Tanhum replies, 'An excellent suggestion. But of course we who are circumcised cannot become like you. So you get circumcised and become like us.'

"'A wise answer,' says the Tsar. 'Unfortunately it is the law that anyone who bests the Tsar in argument must be thrown to the lions.'

"So they threw Rabbi Tanhum to the lions. But the lions stood back and would not attack him. An unbeliever was watching this, and said, 'The reason the lions do not eat him is that they are not hungry.' To test this theory, the Tsar had the unbeliever thrown to the lions. They promptly gobbled him up."

Now there was no mistaking his expression. The warmest of smiles opened, revealing the crookedest of teeth, and Chaim withdrew.

I noticed at dinner that Kevin left his cell off the table. It and his Blackberry usually replaced knife and spoon. I asked him whether there was a parable about Blackberries.

"It's a funny thing. Kayim started in and I told him right off I was here to fish. No God crap. He never said another word.

"So we fished. I got skunked in the morning. Mid-afternoon I foul-hooked a tiny brookie. Meantime he's pulling them in. Not tons, understand, but steady. On a tough day. I'm going nuts.

"Finally, four o'clock, remember our boat has an early day, I can't stand it. I ask him. 'Can you tell me what you're using?'

"He smiles. Reels in. Then he looks at me and asks, 'Can I tell you a story?' Well, I reel in too. There we are, drifting down this canyon, water green and fishy is passing me by.

"At the end of the story he hands me his rod. Goes," and Kevin moves his hand palm up to say, Give it a try. "I look. He's got an attractor nymph up top, a smidge of weight, twelve inches lower a sixteen Caddis emerger. Ties them himself."

"And the story?" Jake and I inched in.

"A man, the only rich man in the village—could have been the same village as your guy, Jake—makes a donation to the little synagogue. The rabbi asks how he is, and he boasts about his business. He never mentions his family, his wife. Only how much money he makes.

"The rabbi thanks the man for the donation and asks him to help with a chore. A nail has worked loose on the rabbi's study bench. He asks the man to hold the bench.

"The rabbi takes a gold watch from the man's pocket and holds it in the palm of his hand. And uses it to drive the nail.

"Well, naturally, the watch shatters. 'What are you doing?' yells the man.

"'You see how ill suited is this tool for the task? The watch has a very different purpose.

"'Tonight when you go home, I want you to spend five minutes looking in the mirror. Look at your eye. Consider how it works. It is more beautiful, more complex than this watch. And it is a single part of the most complex machine in the universe. Ask yourself whether that invention, constructed with such elegance, is good only to make money.'

"'Oh yes. And with your donation, I'm going to buy you a new watch.'

"Then Kayim hands me his rod and tells me if I will also give five minutes to looking in the mirror at my eye, I can fish with his rod the rest of the day.

"I used that rod. Got three good fish before the pull-out."

• • •

I began my day with Chaim as did Kevin, resolved not to discuss the Talmud, life in Poland, or the ways of God to the dry fly. Just to fish.

Chaim was waiting by the put-in when the guide and I drove up, the McKenzie boat lashed to the trailer we pulled. He was in his black suit, the odd tassels, a clean white shirt buttoned at the collar. And of course the encompassing hat. He must have sensed my reluctance to engage, for he said little as we began the float. The guide and I spoke about fishing techniques. Occasionally Chaim chimed in.

We beached midway and Cort set up a field table and chairs for our lunch. He'd brought fried chicken, coleslaw, potato salad, for himself and me. Chaim took a large white kerchief from a pocket and unwrapped it. Bowed his head in prayer. We waited until he finished.

That's when I asked him something personal. I didn't want to be rude, but I was curious.

"Where was I born? What makes you ask?"

"You have an interesting accent."

"I was born in Bronx, New York."

Had I brought up the wrong subject? "Then your accent . . ."

". . . is Yiddish. That is my first language."

"Really. I didn't know it was still spoken."

"A Frenchman speaks French, an Italian speaks Italian. A Jew speaks Jewish."

"I know lots of Jews who don't speak it."

"I know lots of birds who don't fly. Turkeys, do you envy them? Chickens lay eggs for men and foxes to eat."

"Do you have an answer for every question?"

"Did you ask a question?"

I smiled. He had me.

"So you have a rebuttal for every statement."

"For every question, I have a question. For every argument I have an argument."

We fished a while in silence. Every fish I hooked he hooked and landed two. Cort had a quizzical smile on his face. I think I did too.

"Chaim, tell me what 'Hasid' means."

"'Hasid' means pious. Hasidim, the pious ones."

I considered my next comment. I wasn't sure I should make it. "I'm not a pious person." He unleashed a low, flat cast that sped under the overhang of a cottonwood. A fat rainbow took the fly. Chaim didn't respond until the fish had been netted, unhooked, set free.

"The Talmud teaches," he squinted at the sky and I checked to be sure he wasn't reading his lines, "that when you are brought before the heavenly court, God's first question is, 'Did you live a righteous life?' His second question is, 'Did you set aside regular time for study of my word?' What can we conclude from this?"

"I'm not sure."

He shook his finger as if counting a tempo. "It is more important to be righteous than pious," he said immediately.

All the God talk made me nervous. I told him.

"A good sign. We should be nervous in the presence of the Almighty."

He reeled in a little brook trout, all spangles and raspberry spots in a blue halo. "Salvelinus fontinalis," he said to me and held the hook at its bend. The fish slipped free and fell back in the stream untouched.

There were two hunts going on. In one, he and I were hunter, and the fish were prey. In the second, he was deftly leading me, his quarry, through maze and trail, hoping to snare me in a theological discussion. I would play, but on my terms.

I asked about the Hasids. People think, he said, because they dress in black and keep to themselves, Hasidim are dour people. No one, he said, emphasizes more the joy of Creation, the beauty of God's gifts. Sex, he said. It surprised me. "No child is born except through pleasure and joy. Food, drink, this—" and he pointed his clumsy rod at our glorious surroundings.

"So why do they dress in that getup?"

"It honors our founder. And also reminds us that clothes are just a fashion."

For years Hasidim were warned against the "treyfe medina." The outside world, he translated, but I knew it meant the unclean world. But now his people see the benefit in coming out and explaining themselves. That was part of what he was doing on this trip.

"So how do you get to be so proficient an angler, living in the Bronx?"

"Study," he replied as if the answer were obvious. He had started with Isaac Walton. Then the Schwiebert two-volume work. All of Roderick Haig-Brown, all of Joe Brooks. To learn to tie, Jack Dennis and Doug Swisher.

"But you must have done a lot of fishing as well?"

"No. Only this." He let go an S-cast to the bank, configured to let the line absorb two intermediate currents and allow the fly a natural float. It was a perfect cast, and so thought a foot-long brown.

"You didn't learn that from books."

"Books and practice. In the basement of my *shul*—you know that word?" he asked slyly.

"I know that word."

"In the basement is a long room, used for overflow. It has a sixteen-foot ceiling. I was allowed to practice. A book in one hand, the rod in the other. Excellent discipline that ceiling. It keeps your loop low and tight."

"And your gear?"

"Bought from E-Bay. All good values. The rod cost eleven dollars. Plus shipping."

He realized he was being out-maneuvered and turned a question on me.

"Tell me about your work."

So I did. I didn't think God could intrude on American Colonial history, so I told him. Of my studies, my teaching, my paltry research papers. By the end I began to hear the discouragement in my words. Perhaps, I ventured, I'd been at it too long.

"Can one study history too long?" he asked.

"Aren't all things possible?"

He smiled. "Well, my friend. I too study history. I study four or five hours every day. And every day the same book. Have I been at it too long?

"And to answer your question. Yes indeed. All things are possible. But only if you recognize the Force that creates possibilities."

His Sabbath ended at sunset, on the river, and there was a prayer for that. Afterwards, we were in Cort's SUV, pulling the McKenzie and bouncing along rutted dirt roads. Cort was telling us how the valley had been settled by LDS families during the great Emigration. I was in the front seat, Chaim behind. At a break, I turned to him. He had more to say.

"You believe you are not pious. Do you know what the word means?"

"Religious."

"That is a second meaning. Its first meaning is Dedicated. You are dedicated to your family and your studies."

"I suppose I am."

"So you are pious. Yet you still sometimes feel lonely and empty."

"Did I say that?"

"Did you have to? I think you wonder about who you are."

"Don't you?"

"Now it is you who answer a question with a question. There is an old saying . . ."

"Why am I not surprised?"

". . . that when two people become friends, they make two souls against a single body. Bodies are self-centered—each pursues its own needs. Two souls can join forces. I am writing down for you my telephone number. You call me. We will find an hour every Thursday to discuss. Our talk will nourish two souls, give focus to two lives. You will see."

I took the paper, crumpled it, and stuck it in my vest. I had no intention of using it.

• • •

Bright and early Sunday morning, after a breakfast of steak, fried eggs, and cowboy coffee, we said our goodbyes. We thanked Mrs. Henders and tipped her heavily to compensate for Jake's change of heart. A somewhat bewildered Sherree hung back. We stuffed our gear into the trunk of the rental car and speculated whether we'd have a chance to say goodbye to Chaim. Sure enough, on cue, he appeared.

Somehow the perpetual eclipse under the hat had dissipated. Maybe it was the long-slanting morning light, a maizey reflection off the freshly mowed alfalfa fields, but you could actually see his face. He seemed younger, and—funny what a day in a boat can do—he looked like someone we'd known a long time.

He carried his fishing gear. "I want you to know you have made this trip a memorable one for me. After all, I am not what you expected, and I can not replace your missing companion." Since we'd met Chaim, no one had mentioned Ed. "I shall always remember you."

We were to a man embarrassed. Kevin mumbled something about paths crossing and I thought to say how much meeting him had meant to us, but didn't. Jake offered a ride to the airport.

"No thank you. Cort drives me to Boise for my bus."

"Bus? To the Bronx?"

"Actually the East Side Terminal. Manhattan."

"How long does that take?"

"Two days, fourteen hours." We blinked in unison. No one asked whether it was ritual, economy, or preference. "Do you know," he asked, "there is a town in Wyoming called Little America? I hope to see it, although we stop there at three thirty in the morning.

"I want to make gifts to you." He handed Jake his fly box. Inside three-dozen flies, dry and nymph, every one hand-tied, were lined up in the ridged foam in size places. Chaim's flies were works of art, you could hang the collection on the wall like a shadow-box. I envied Jake his gift.

Then he gave Kevin his reel. It was a tinny, simple thing, a gift perhaps with a message, since Kevin had only the newest and best of everything. His own reel was a large arbor, block-cast aluminum model that twenty of Chaim's would not have bought.

And to me he handed his rod, a thick, awkward stick that in his hands had been a wand of grace.

"To you," he said in his stiff, old-world way. "The pious angler."

Cort threw the black satchel in back of the pick-up, and Chaim folded his shrouded frame into the front seat. What, I wondered, would they talk of? Would Cort tell him of his doubts with the fantastical story of Joseph Smith and the invisible golden tablets, the magical lenses, the visit of the Angel Moroni? Or would they talk hatches?

I left that paper in my vest the rest of the season. It was December before I pulled it out, January before I used it. I don't think I've missed half a dozen Thursdays since. I've become fanatical about that conversation, where ethics, diet, history, God, ritual, joy, observance and culture are discussed. Every once in a while, Chaim asks about fishing.

HEAD ON

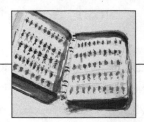

THE LAST SEASON

He used the river the way some used a first love. He could always dredge it up and let the memory of it salve his thoughts. It was in his mind when he heard a match strike or a Hank Williams song; it was in his mind when he drove about idly on errands, for they were always errands that reminded him of people no longer here, and that recollection brought back the river.

This day he drove up to see it, an early March day that had spring tucked far up its sleeve, so cold he doubted he would fish. It was cold and damp. He told himself if he fished at all he would stand on the bank. City fishing, Fitz used to call it.

Electric lights showed in windows of the small frame houses, people still at home. Local folk. On a winter morning, after elk season and before the first warmth brought out the fishermen, local folk stayed at home. With no tourists, there was no sense opening up the hardware store, the tackle shop, the filling station. They stayed inside, poured a third cup of coffee. Talked to each other about what was in the newspaper and listened to the radio, that fellow who made fun of politicians.

Driving up he visualized profiles of the river. The deep oxbow where Fitz had taken that large cutthroat, the riffle by the fallen barn, the gravel bed where whitefish gathered and dappled the water with their distinctive takes. The electric lights added cheer to his drive. Grains of snow flicked at the windshield and gathered in pockets along the road like dust balls. Cars came driving downhill toward town, and their wake blew apart the white clumps. Stopped at a traffic light, he noticed how the sparrows on the wire were puffing themselves up, against the wind. He was warm in the car, but seeing them pull their heads into their feathers gave him a shiver, and he cranked the heater up a notch. Colder, Fitz would have said, colder than a titch's wit. He and Fitz had driven this stretch of road a hundred times. Towards the end, Fitz had stayed home, and we'd fished solo.

His daughter had asked him not to go. Shouldn't be wading alone, not at your age. You could slip, you'd have trouble getting to the car. The way she said it, stern and final in that teacher's voice, suggested it had happened. He saw himself frozen to the shore, his fly line flagging in the current. Never catch a fish that way, he scolded his imagined corpse. Tighten up that slack, control the line.

She was just like her mother. Give her half a chance she saw the dark side. Not at your age. What else was he supposed to do at his age?

He passed the Heavenly Rest Motel and turned right, towards the canyon. Not many late sleepers at the Heavenly Rest. Their trade was never there in the morning. They specialized in early risers, afternoon quickies, and traveling salesmen. Were there still traveling salesmen? Either way, early risers. He smiled at his joke. Then he snorted in phlegm that stuck at the back of his head to free his breathing, rolled down the window and spat. It was a gesture that used to drive Betsy mad. Spat across the cold wind and left the window down until he was chilled to shivering.

Where might he start? The large boulder that they had named Charles De Gaulle. Brown trout gathered in its ebb, not big fish, but you could always pick up a brookie there. Why Fitz had given it that name he'd forgotten, if he ever knew. It had no profile, but it rose magisterially out of the black water, like a tombstone. Fitz had been in the European Theater, and he admired De Gaulle. A soldier's soldier. Maybe he would fish the pasture. The wading was easy and the river formed a single curving channel with fish that hove to its bottom awaiting the hatch. When the trout weren't feeding on top, they were lined up in the vee of the channel, the mess hall they'd called it.

Or he could try the Drop, the sudden shelf made by God knows what where the bottom fell off five feet. Once, giving ground to a running fish he'd ended up in the Drop, his waders filling fast. Fitz had pulled him out. He was soaked through, and he stripped down buck naked to dry in the air. He and Fitz were having lunch when the drakes started to hatch. Fitz always said he wished he had a picture. Him in nothing but his boots, not even skivvies, casting into the afternoon hatch.

The pasture was safest. If his daughter knew, she'd insist on the pasture.

The pull-off was webbed over with weeds. It looked as if no one had driven through since last season. Foxtail and buffalo grass whispered against the underside of the truck as he rolled to the trail head. He went through the ritual of rigging and threading his rod, choosing a tippet and tying it on, picking the flies. He had prepared the flies at home. He'd set the large magnifying glass on the dining room table and threaded each fly on tippet. Then tied perfection loops in their end, so all that was left was to join the loops together or separate them out when he wanted to change flies. Carried the snelled flies in an old leather wallet, their lines dangling like the last leaves of autumn. Perhaps he would take a fish home.

He pulled on his hippers, zipped his fleece coat to the chin, and tugged its collar about his ears. Then he started down the path. The wading staff was Fitz's; Fitz had willed it to him along with a box of streamers and three cane rods that Fitz had wound himself. He could never bring himself to use the rods. But the staff, well, for one thing, he needed it here. Hell, he needed it on his front lawn.

Perhaps he would take one home. Pan-size, Betsy used to say. Don't bring me those big footballs you and Fitz lie about. They *taste* like footballs. But pan-sized, that's when they're tender. Whenever he took one for her, he kept a second for himself, and Betsy would fry them for breakfast. He hadn't killed a fish since. Betsy would douse them in buttermilk and roll them in corn meal and cracked pepper, then fire them in a hot skillet, salt and butter, and serve them with a fried tomato. They weren't bad. He never much cared for fish. But every time she served them she would say, fresh as the stream itself, and he liked to hear her say that. She would pick the last daubs of meat from the skeleton with her fingers.

The river was just as he remembered it. While he studied its unreadable surface, a chickadee pipped away in the bordering pines. The snows started again, this time flakes the size of dimes, and wet. He jammed his hands in his pockets and caught the rod under his arm. There was a shed downstream, and he decided to sit for a while to see where the weather was going. Weather's always going, Fitz used to say. Trouble is, there's weather right behind it.

The shed was warm and smelled of mice and old newspaper. Inside was an old rocker, its woven bottom tired and frayed, and a stump someone had hauled in to sit on. He chose the stump, and stuck his booted feet out as if they were warming by a fire. Leaned back against the raw planks of the wall. He was short of breath from the walk and he could hear his heart. That'll happen more and more, the doctor had warned. You can't push it. What the hell do doctors know? That's what Fitz and he had asked each other angrily about what they told Betsy and later about what they told Fitz. What the hell do they know? The answer is, they were right both times. Fitz would have laughed at that. Turns out they did know.

He looked down to see what he'd put on. Two soft-hackle flies, each on its separate snell. Fished together, they get more attention. That was an old-fashioned way, two wet flies. He'd drift them down and begin his retrieve on the quarter. Let them swing downstream and gather the line in his left hand, working it like a rug hooker to spindle in the line so they'd come back slow. That way you'd feel a take. Now if he was going to switch to dries, he'd use those big Grey Wulffs. He couldn't see anything these days much smaller than a strawberry. He thought of how Fitz had organized his fly box. Flies lined up like a squadron, like they were ready to go to war. Fitz would talk to them as he tied them on. You're going under for your country, just remember that. Hold your breath and keep your eyes peeled. You get a chance at that fish's lip, hold tight. We'll be right behind you, we'll bail you out. But until we do, your job is to hold on.

Or his speech when he'd retire a fly. You've done great service, he'd say. For duty above and beyond, he'd say, and replace the sodden fly in its rank. When a fly came apart or the point of its hook broke, he'd speak to it of noble deeds, cut it loose, and toss it on the waters. Then he'd pucker his lips like a trumpet and pipe taps. Pa-pa-pa. A military burial.

He smiled and rose. Outside the snow had stopped and the light had brightened. He blew into his fists and went out the door.

Down by the pasture, there was not a trace of life. The river could be empty for all it showed; the planet could be abandoned. He watched for several minutes but nothing changed. Still standing on the bank, he let out a first cast. That was something he could always do, cast a fly line. Fitz used to say when you go, leave that to me, will you? The wind was coming downstream and he wanted to get his line quartered up for the drift, so he tightened his loop and dropped his hands at the end of the cast. The line peeled out, as he'd intended, sailed with a little over-shoot so that when it landed, soft as air, slack fell with the flies. That way they started to dive before the current began to move them downstream. He made several casts to cover the water on the near side, retrieving each methodically. Then rolled a bow of line out, picked up the line, and cast again.

Water has an enduring memory. The currents follow what has happened before, the streams drape the same rocks, the same banks. The river remembers, will not change until some part of its foundation changes. A boulder gives, a rotted trunk falls, a pebble on the streambed. Otherwise the water remembers, and the river does what it did.

Cast again. This time to the far side. As soon as the line straightened and just as his fingers thought to tighten the swing, a fish hit. He played it easily, with respect.

The fish ran deep and he lifted the rod tip to put pressure on it. It jumped in the gray light and jumped again. That's tiring for you, he thought. Your breath will go short and you'll hear your heart. Pretty soon you'll need to sit down.

Sure enough the fish played itself out. He reeled it close and with his left hand lifted it out of the water. It wasn't a large fish. Its back was black tending to green, along its side the telltale rayon-pink chevron of the rainbow, all against a glittering silver. He lifted the hook from its lip. Ten inches, maybe a little more. Pan-size, he thought.

He fetched a pocket knife from his jeans. Propped the fish against a rock and, holding the nacre handle of the knife between thumb and finger, loosely, so it would swing, delivered a single downward blow to the fish that dispatched its life. As soon as he struck, he wished he hadn't. The trout faded. The brilliance of its skin disappeared and its eye went to stone. The colors faded into the colorless breeze. Why, he wondered, did I do that? What do I have now?

He unfolded the main blade, making to clean the fish. But as soon as he turned it over, its white, lifeless belly, the useless fins, the dark spot of the anus, he felt queasy. He had gutted maybe a thousand trout in his days. He would scatter the entrails for hawks, wash out the slick cavity in the river bottom and scrub the blood from his hands with river sand. But he had cleaned his last fish. This one he left by the rock in the pasture.

It wouldn't be wasted. A magpie had settled in a stunted pine across the stream to watch him land it. The bird was waiting for him to move on.

You have to be careful. The magic of the fish can only be glimpsed in the stream, the doe amongst the trees. What's transient is lasting. Nothing else. It was a deep knowledge, painful and tugging like a hook stuck in his gut.

He sat for a while on the rocks of the bank, not wanting to leave. He let his feet dangle in the current. The boots bobbed about with their own life. The ground was littered with the husks of last year's cover, grasses turned to straw, and brittle. A single weed stood tall among the dead thistle. Its spike of seeds had frozen on the stalk. Once he had known its name, but he couldn't remember anymore. That's what happens. One by one you learn the names, then one by one you forget them.

While he dreamed, the magpie flew down. It startled him with a great cry. He looked up to see it drive its bonehard beak into the stomach of the dead fish.

Odd about that fish's eye. It didn't show fear when he'd reeled it close; it didn't show anything. If the eyes are the windows of the soul, he couldn't see in. That eye was either on or off, like a traffic light. Do fish have a soul? Do they go to heaven? If they don't, heaven has barren streams. That would piss off Fitz. Long way to go to get skunked. Whenever they would quit, they'd sit by the bank for a while and slug Canadian whiskey from a flask. A drink, Fitz would say, makes me feel like a new man. Trouble is, then the new man wants a drink. He'd say it every time.

• • •

At home, he was watching the evening news when his daughter called. She called every evening, to make sure he was alive.

"How was the fishing?" she asked.

"Good," he said absently. "The fishing was good."

"How many did you get?"

"One," he said.

"One? One, and the fishing was good? That must have been some fish."

"Yes," he told her in a voice steady and clear. "It was some fish."

JT

ACKNOWLEDGMENTS

Much of this material first appeared elsewhere, including in *Gray's Sporting Journal* ("The Specter at Grizzly Hackle"); *Big Sky Journal* ("On Dry Land," "The Green Lantern," and "The Home Pool"); *Icarus* ("Ute Creek Pass"); *High Country Angler* ("I Can Prove It" and "What He Sees"); and in two of my novels, *Marital Assets* (Sag Harbor, NY: Permanent Press, 1994) and *Mooney in Flight* (San Francisco, CA: Macadam/Cage, 2003). "The Tarpon on the Wall" is included in the story anthology *For the Defense*. The main character from "The View from Buffalo Mountain" appears, with new name, toes, and story, in *Dizzying Heights: The Aspen Novel* (Fulcrum Books 2008). Thanks to all for permission to reprint here.

Macallan Distilleries, Easter Elchies, Scotland, awarded "I Can Prove It" its grand prize. My thanks to them for the recognition and for their excellent whisky.

FiN.